A History of
THE CHRISTIAN CHURCH
AND CHURCH OF
CHRIST IN MINNESOTA

By

ADA L. FORSTER

CHRISTIAN BOARD OF PUBLICATION
St. Louis, Missouri
1953

Dedicated to my mother
SARAH JANE HANCOCK FORSTER
whose inspiration led her five children
into Christian service.

Miss Ada L. Forster, author of "History of the Disciples
of Christ in Minnesota."

Famous Minnehaha Falls,

      Minneapolis, Minnesota.

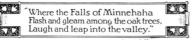

"Where the Falls of Minnehaha
Flash and gleam among the oak trees,
Laugh and leap into the valley."

—Longfellow

Introduction to the Author

Ada L. Forster was a preacher. She was much besides—an efficient administrator, a tireless secretary, a lover of the brotherhood of the Disciples of Christ, and, above all, a great soul. Her leadership in Minnesota was characterized by an unwearying persistence that never counted the odds. Her Christian influence ever revealed "the light of the knowledge of the glory of God" as it shone for her "in the face of Jesus Christ." Minnesota Disciples will not be skimpy in their tributes to the part "Miss Ada" has played in the making of the history about which she has so interestingly written.

Miss Forster was born in Birkenhead, England. She was baptized by J. M. Van Horn, an Ohio minister, affiliating with the Alvanley Place Church of Christ in Birkenhead. She began her labors in Minnesota in 1907, being ordained to the Christian ministry in the Garden City church. Her first pastorate was with the Fairmont church.

When the Christian Woman's Board of Missions needed a field worker in the "central north" Miss Forster accepted their invitation to larger work and led the women in our Christian churches in four states. Later she became the trusted and competent state secretary for Minnesota and the Dakotas. She closed her Minnesota labors in Minneapolis with a ten-year pastorate in the Minnehaha church, 1935-1945.

It takes far more than an introduction to remind readers of Miss Forster's labors in preparing for and conducting conventions, leading in evangelistic projects, and promoting missionary and educational programs. With dignity, sincerity, and distinction she has imparted inspiration, faith and strength to innumerable Christian people and churches. No living person is as well qualified to write a "History of the Christian Church and Church of Christ in Minnesota" as Ada L. Forster. She has demonstrated a remarkable power to command the

5

respect and affection of Minnesota Disciples because she has lived effectually in an outstandingly Christian fashion.

Although Miss Forster's history looks back, it invites, encourages and even challenges Disciples today to a more significant dedication to the "Faith of Our Fathers." Her chapters will contribute to a cooperative and unified brotherhood to which Miss Ada's whole life and ministry have been so joyously given. Her love and faithfulness are the essence of our religion and the hope of our world.

Forrest L. Richeson
Minneapolis, Minnesota

Foreword

In writing the history of Minnesota churches, we must needs give a brief picture of the land to which the pioneers came with their message of what has been called: "The Restoration Movement of the Nineteenth Century."

Historical records show that Minnesota had Territorial standing early in the Nineteenth Century. In 1857 the Government purchased land in the St. Croix, Stillwater area, from St. Croix Indians and from that time white settlers were to be found, chiefly in lumber camps.

There were three Territorial Governors in the nine years, from 1849 to 1858. It was in 1849 that the real movement of white people to the new country began. Just six years later we find the testimony of the pioneers of our church.

This North Star State, with its more than ten thousand lakes, its hills and prairies, was the thirty-second State to be received into the Union, on May 12, 1858. By that time our pioneers had held two "State Meetings," their first one being in 1856, making the year of Statehood the beginning of their third year of work. One can have some idea of the joy of these State gatherings, since the new churches were far apart. A quarterly report of one of the evangelists, T. T. Van Dolah, gives some idea of early effort. We quote: "Travelled by team 450 miles, preached 45 discourses, had 55 additions, 17 by letter and 38 by obedience."

From Encyclopeadia Britannica we find that the Federal census of 1860 shows that the population was 172,023, also that Minnesota supplied over 25,000 men for the Federal armies in the Civil War, when men were needed to defend their new homes.

Few and far apart our people served and still kept in touch with each other. Cold and heat, poor means of travel, small means of livelihood, could not prevent them from planting churches.

From family histories and early stories of pioneers we know that danger from Indians came to their homes. In 1857 and 1862 there were Indian uprisings, 1862 being the date of the last serious trouble.

From the families of Lucius and Fillmore Mills, who settled in 1854, as small boys with their parents, Mr. and Mrs. Samuel

7

Mills, about two miles from Garden City, we learn that their neighbors were all Indians, no other white people having yet settled near them. These Indians would crowd into the Mills' home until no more could get in. Mrs. Mills had great courage in dealing with them. Unusually friendly, they could easily become angry. The little boys of that day told their grandchildren seventy years later of a time when an Indian became angry with their mother, picked up a gun to strike her, but meeting her unflinching eyes as they rested upon him, dropped his weapon and walked out.

This family, with others of southern Minnesota, left home in 1862, in the Sioux Indian uprising. Southern Minnesota and part of Iowa were affected. A family named Jewett, living near Garden City, was supposedly all killed, but the youngest child was afterward found alive. He recovered and grew up.

A strange Indian resting place was discovered in this section. Noticing numerous large flies at an intended picnic, an investigation was made. Three Indians had been given their last resting place on rude scaffolds, laid high in a clump of oak trees.

Also in 1862, George S. and Susan Fowler, living near our present Horian Church, Martin County, and afterwards members of that church, were warned by a horseman from Mankato that the Indians were traveling, painted and angry. George nailed willow branches over a democrat wagon, emptied a straw mattress over these ribs, placed a feather bed on top and took his wife and three-week-old son, Herbert, away from the danger zone. George returned in a short time to find his home in ashes, but Susan and her baby could not return for some time, since her health was impaired. Herbert was a deacon in the Fairmont church when we knew him. Friendly Indians called him "Puckachee," when he was a lad, which means "to skedaddle."

Surely "many adversaries" surrounded the pioneers, but their faith was greater than all of them.

Ada L. Forster

Contents

Historic Personalities of Minnesota Churches

Some great churches of the Christian family have celebrated their Centennials in Minnesota in 1950, among them the Methodist Church.

While the Disciples of Christ are not as strong in Minnesota as in many other states, we can claim almost as early a date for the beginning of our mission as many of them. It seems well established that in 1855, about six years after the first white settlers came to the state, there came those who carried the message of the Campbells, Stone, Scott and others. With heroic courage they preached in their new home.

We will not attempt to give reasons why our growth has not been greater. You may read between the lines and supply some of them. Perhaps the coming of many German and Scandinavian settlers, with their Luthern churches, is one reason.

Your historian must needs speak in the first person in introducing these pioneers, since she is passing on their words to you. To her, brought up in our British churches and having heard some of our great American ministers, E. M. Todd, J. M. Van Horn, J. J. Haley, J. H. Garrison, A. McLean, F. M. Rains and others, it was a great privilege to meet laymen and women who had planted their faith in the new country.

My first acquaintance with Minnesota churches came in 1907, at the annual Convention held in Portland Avenue Church, Minneapolis. It was there I met some who were growing old, but who had planted churches in earlier days. Impressed by their faith, hope and love I talked often with these dear people. Their courage in bringing the "Restoration" movement to Minnesota has added greatly to the whole Christian message in the North Star State.

GEORGE TANNER

An elder in the Fairmont church, to which I ministered, he neither preached nor evangelized. As I mentioned Alexander Campbell, he raised his right hand reverently and said, "I heard him." Others of those whose preaching belonged to the

11

same season he heard also. He told his young minister of
hearing the Message of Christ in the Brush Run Church, how
the building would be crowded, how folk would sit outside on
the window sills and crowd close to the building, all anxious to
hear. Part of his eldership was to be sure the preacher understood the "Plea" of the Disciples of Christ. He was 90 years
old when I knew him, but well able to explain his Faith. The
Lord's Table was a MUST with him. "Ruling" elders had
their great uses in those days.

DAVID M. HAGGARD

From Dr. George D. Haggard, now 96 years old and living
in Minneapolis, Minnesota, we have some of the particulars of
the ministry of his father, David M. Haggard. Dr. George
Haggard has been an elder in the Portland Avenue Church in
Minneapolis for more than half a century and though he is
now unable to leave his home his interest as an elder is as great
as ever. Mildreth J. Haggard of the Tipi Wakan story is his
daughter.

In 1857 David M. Haggard resided near Eau Claire, Wisconsin. He knew that Christian Church services were being held
in Pleasant Grove, in the home of David Overend. Later three
of the Haggard brothers moved to Fairpoint, two miles from
Old Concord. In May, 1857, David Haggard, with Mary his
wife, started a 20-mile drive to attend services, using an ox
team. As they were skirting a lake the oxen decided to take
a rest, walked into the lake and stayed there. The oxen had
"mule" dispositions, evidently. David, with his wife, Mary, and
their five-month-old son, George D. Haggard, had to wade out
of the water and continue on foot, baby George riding on his
father's shoulder. They arrived in time for worship, the oxen
following later when it suited them.

In 1870 we read that David Haggard was called to hold a
meeting for the church at Mantorville. There were thirty-three
(33) converts baptized in the stream three miles distant, a
hole being cut in the ice to provide this outdoor baptistry.
We think there must have been, in those days, companies of
people meeting in homes. We have no account of a church
building being erected in many places mentioned.

In 1877-1880 Mr. Haggard lived at Springfield, Brown
County. He preached at Canby (doubtless among the Antelope

Hills group) and at other churches in southern Minnesota. Whenever he passed through Mankato he preached there. Like many others, he was known as "Elder" and did not receive salary.

We have also heard of Nancy Jane Haggard Smith, daughter of David M., who lived at Concord. At the time of her death she was 100 years and seven months old.

Mrs. John Truax and Mrs. Esperance LaDow

Two dear ladies of some 80 years old sat one day in the home of Mrs. LaDow's daughter, Mrs. Frank Latham, in the pretty town of Howard Lake. They were singing from a strange-looking hymnbook. They told me it had been used in Minnesota in the day of early evangelism of John Truax and others. Most of the hymns had many verses. They were singing the words—

> "Methinks I hear some sinner say, Let me go,
> I'll start at once, so clear the way; Let me go.
> My earthly friends I say farewell,
> I will not go with you to hell,
> I start at once with Christ to dwell:
> Let me go; fare you well."

Their eyes glistened as they told how many, many people "came down the aisle on that verse." They talked of Pleasant Grove, Marion and Antelope Hills churches, all of which have at some time claimed to be the FIRST CHURCH organized in Minnesota. My own belief is that these churches came into being at dates very close to each other. They told me stories of sacrifice, preachers walking miles and miles, accepting hospitality of brethren, never knowing what they might receive to sustain their families; of how wives and children kept home fires burning by their own effort, but always rejoicing in the fact that it was for the gospel's sake. Yet these ladies were young looking for their age, trim and beautiful to see, their faces filled with joy and peace. They were talking of Civil War days and of Soldiers of the Cross who were "holding the fort" for men who were to return to Minnesota and make homes.

These good women told of early conventions in Minnesota. Such gatherings were times of great fellowship. Many would drive for several days to the chosen place. They prepared for weeks ahead, getting their provisions ready. Then, sometimes driving ox teams, hitched to democrat wagons, they would take the family along.

Arriving at the convention place, these people would put their food together and have one great picnic at each meal. Sometimes they killed their meat on the spot. Families were very hospitable; people living close to the convention gave their best. With the bedding each family would bring, the homes opened would crowd women and children into one room and the men and boys in another. They would, of course, make their beds on the floor.

These conventions were high points in the church life, highly prized times of communion and the place of planning for future evangelism.

Mr. and Mrs. A. P. Frost and Adelaide Gail Frost

I first met this wonderful family in 1908. Adelaide was home on one of her furloughs from our India Mission. They were living at that time on the J. R. Watkins' estate. (The well-known Watkin's Medical Supplies Company.) After our State Convention in Winona, I had the blessing of being a guest of the Frosts with the honored Alexander McLain. We talked of India and of someone needed to go back with Adelaide. Had not some circumstances prevented at that time I would have offered.

The home was beautiful with love and Christian purpose. Mrs. Frost and Adelaide were round, comfortable, homelike persons. On this occasion Mrs. Frost was in the kitchen preparing the shortcake for the strawberries the other members of the family and the guests were picking in the garden. She was a great housekeeper. Adelaide was the kind of person who never ceased to give information about India in her conversation. Our India Mission lived in her and she loved her friends in that land. Mr. Frost was tall, spare, with flashing eyes, a dry humor and a quick repartee. Their whole life and thinking was of the ongoing of the Kingdom of God.

Mr. Frost was educated the hard way, chiefly by his own reading and research from his boyhood days. He was a great preacher. I learned that in Civil War days he had pioneered in Minnesota in many of our older churches and that Adelaide was baptized while he was ministering to the Concord church. During my Fairmont ministry they lived in Mankato and I was frequently in their home, intensely interested in Minnesota History. Mr. Frost was fond of discussion and was often heard on the floor of our conventions. He never could sympathize with ministers who could not stand hardship and who were not able to wrestle with problems. On one occasion he said that many preachers refused to stay in Minnesota, that they "came in with the birds in the spring and went out with the geese in the fall; perhaps the FROSTS nipped them."

He had been a great contender in doctrinal matters and a stalwart proponent of the position of the Disciples of Christ. A short time before his death he said to me, "Ada, preach in love; sometimes I have contended too hard for what I believed, but only the love I put into my sermons remains for me now." His sense of humor never left him. That day he said, "Let's get away from this mundane world and make a sermon." At that point Mrs. Frost entered the room. Being very deaf she could not hear our conversation. It being almost lunch time, she said, "Alva, what will it be, baked beans, cold meat, custard pudding?" At that juncture Mr. Frost replied, "Angels and ministers of grace preserve us, you have brought us right back to this old world."

It was in longer conversation with the family that I knew of their deprivation. They had lived in a shack during winter days. Mrs. Frost had taken the quilts from the beds in the daytime to hang them over the cracks in the wall, that the small stove might sufficiently warm the house. They had little money, just what the folk who were poor could give them. Most of what little money they had was used in travel. A high chair was cherished by them, because they had bought it for Adelaide by not eating butter and eggs. There was the "story of the shirt," as I called it. Six dollars was paid for pants that were new, but there was no coat for the preacher to wear. Some material was found to make a shirt and the preacher pretended he did not like to wear a coat when he preached. They walked miles, rode horseback sometimes, and buggies were a luxury. It was Mrs. Frost who organized the State Christian Woman's Board of Missions in Minnesota, during the State Convention in 1880 in the Pleasant Grove church. She was the first State President. I remember that in one convention, about 1910, in that same

church, she told of the early days and the rearing of that building, adding, "Young folks, we have done this, but it is for
you to keep the roof on, the windows in, and to make this place
greater than ever."

MRS. MARY OVEREND

I went into the home of this interesting woman on one fall
evening. She led me into a comfortable room, feather bed and
all, bringing with her the wash water for the visitor. Looking
down at me from the walls were the GREAT FOUR, Thomas
and Alexander Campbell, Walter Scott, Barton Stone and there
were other pictures of later leaders, as well as of the family.
I was precipitated into the past as my hostess began at once
to tell of early days. She told how her husband walked 75
miles to find a minister. He was David Overend, leader in the
Pleasant Grove church. She remarked that ministers of the
early days did not require a room, or wash water in their room,
that times had changed. She was showing me every courtesy
and did not mean to begrudge the kindness, she simply wanted
me to know their history.

CHARLES B. OSGOOD

On May 22, 1934, Charles B. Osgood was called to the "House
of Many Mansions." He had spent a little more than a year as
minister of the church in Castle Rock, Washington.

Though Mr. Osgood was of later date, he must be regarded as
a pioneer. He came to the State from Ohio in 1899. He was a
graduate of Hiram College. He served in Minnesota for thirty-
four years. His entire ministry was forty-five years. His first
pastorate in Minnesota was in the Grand Avenue Church in
Minneapolis. Other pastorates were in Winona and Mankato.

Mr. Osgood was called to the State work at a time when an
aggressive program had not been carried on for some years.
He held the office of State Secretary-Evangelist, that of Regional Secretary of Minnesota and the Dakotas, and finally of
City Missionary in Minneapolis, during his Minnesota service.

Charlie, as he was known to many, never thought of his own
comfort. In very person and situation he thought of the
possibilities of betterment. During his regional secretarial
days he traveled, seldom going into diners. He would eat
sack lunch for whole days. On trains he sat up at night to

save the expense of a berth. He felt he must save missionary money. His co-workers continually asked him to make himself comfortable, but he always smiled and said, "I am all right." He was one of the most patient men to be found anywhere and full of kindness for his friends in all the churches.

Through the years he knew the families of the churches as intimately as did their own ministers. Many of the churches he served for long periods, straightening out tangles and leaving them with ministers. To Disciples living in towns where they did not have their own church he became pastor-at-large. A Minneapolis businessman said of him: "Charlie never knows when a church is dead." With him no situation was ever "dead."

The Grand Avenue Church in Minneapolis was discontinued at a time when Mr. Osgood was evangelizing in South Dakota. His spirit of love and reverence was shown as he came into the regional office in Minneapolis and said to the secretary: "I've been to old Grand Avenue; I stood on the steps with my hat off and said to my God that if I could only have had two good years there, the Grand Avenue Christian Church sign would still have been up." He frequently stood with his God on "holy ground."

Mr. Osgood's son and daughters belonged to another Christian communion after they grew up. He rejoiced that his son Howard became a missionary in Tibet for the Assemblies of God Church, and that his two daughters, Julia and Ruth, used their beautiful voices for evangelistic singing. So lived the man who sang and preached the gospel longer than any other minister in Minnesota.

Your historian's first State Convention in Minnesota was in 1907. There was a great family spirit at that time and much joy in the churches as they carried their part of the brotherhood's world Missions. There was also outstanding leadership in the work of Mr. and Mrs. A. D. Harmon, Mr. and Mrs. A. P. Frost, J. H. Bicknell, Mr. and Mrs. Perry J. Rice, Mr. F. H. Mellen, Mr. and Mrs. Charles Oliver, Miss Florence Pierce, and many very wonderful leaders. Other leaders of our churches will be mentioned as the history of the churches unfolds.

May all who in this day build upon their foundation be worthy of them.

The Minnesota Christian Education Association

In 1871 Austin B. Council, of Mankato, passed away and with his passing a dream of a Christian College for Minnesota and the Northwest was retarded for a time. It had been the aim of the pioneers to have such a college, in which ministers and Christian workers could be trained. Mr. Council left a sum of money, known as the A. B. Council Fund, which was invested for educational purposes.

In 1884-1885 the Minnesota Christian Education Association was organized. It became a Minnesota Corporation November 13, 1889. This association worked within the Minnesota Christian Missionary Society.

The purpose of the Association is stated as follows: "The purpose and general nature of the Association shall be the promotion of the educational interest of the State of Minnesota and the territory adjacent or tributary thereto, along the lines of Christian Unity as outlined and exemplified in the teachings of Jesus Christ and his Apostles, and of Christian education in accordance with such unity and teaching. The work shall mainly be done by the establishment, conduct and maintenance of schools and academies, but more especially by the establishment, conduct and maintenance of a college or university of learning; and all such schools and academies, and the college, shall be for the general purpose of instructing, under Christian influences, youth of both sexes, in those branches of knowledge usually taught in similar institutions of the same grades and character in the United States of America.

"The amount of authorized capital stock of the Association is $200,000, divided into 2000 shares of $100 each."

The article of DIRECTORSHIP is as follows: "The management of the corporation is vested in a Board of Directors, consisting of not less than twelve, nor more than twenty stockholders of the corporation. They shall serve without compensation. At least two-thirds of the members of the Board must be members of the Church of Christ, in good and regular standing. One fourth of the members of the Board will be elected at each annual meeting of the stockholders in June, and hold their offices for four years."

At the time of the beginning of the Northwestern Christian College in Excelsior there is this note, concerning the Association's funds: "A considerable majority of the shares of stock subscribed are in the name of the Minnesota Christian Missionary Society, and are voted out as that society directs."

Northwestern Christian College
Excelsior, Minnesota

From Dr. Frank H. Marshall, of Enid, Oklahoma, we have most of our knowledge of the Northwestern Christian College. This was a brave adventure. A building was purchased in Excelsior and years of service anticipated. The College was opened in 1891 and its end came in a tragic way in 1896.

The building purchased by the Minnesota Christian Education Association had been used as a Bible College, known as "Excelsior Institute," and organized by Rev. Charles Galpin in 1857. In 1872 it became "Excelsior Academy" which organization maintained work until 1888-1889. It was a good plant for a small college. The campus was ten acres. Several other "Academy" lots were also purchased at that time.

The Inaugural Assembly of the College was a great event. It was held July 13-19, 1891. The place of the meetings was the Congregational Church in Excelsior. The Mayor of the town gave a welcome, as did many pastors of other local churches. Giving addresses were B. B. Tyler, pastor of the Central Christian Church in New York and eastern editor of the Christian Standard; Charles Louis Loos, President of Kentucky University; Archibald McLean, President of Bethany College and Secretary of the Foreign Christian Missionary Society. Two of the men who served as presidents were Lewis A. Pier and Albert Buxton.

Bachelor of Arts graduates of whom we know, during the short career of the College, were Mr. and Mrs. Ben Shoemaker (parents of Gertrude Shoemaker, Missionary to Africa); Ernest Thornquist, minister; Lee Ferguson, minister; William Reeves, later Professor at Cotner and Phillips. Mr. Shoemaker did much good work in Minnesota. Only Mrs. Alice Wray Shoemaker and Lee Ferguson, of this group, now survive.

Maude W. Waite, of the Garden City church, was a student of Northwestern College. She was married to Frank Marshall,

who was trustee, teacher and vice-president of the College
during all its history. Mr. Marshall served in Minnesota,
ministering in Garden City, Willow Creek and Mankato during the same period in which he gave leadership in the College.
Mr. and Mrs. Marshall were for a time missionaries to Japan.
In later years they have been well known in education. Mrs.
Marshall gained her degree, A.B., at Texas Christian University.

Marshall Building, now being completed, is the newest building of Phillips University. Dr. Marshall was for 34 years Dean
of the Bible College at Phillips and is on the teaching staff still,
making his record at that university over 42 years. He has
given 55 years to our colleges. He and Mrs. Marshall have continued in church school teaching to this day. His ministry has
extended over 64 years. At 82 years old he teaches, preaches
and writes.

Among the directors of the college were John Truax, a
pioneer evangelist; Will U. Smith, layman of the First Christian Church in St. Paul, husband of Mrs. L. Madge Smith; W.
J. Lhamon, minister of Portland Avenue Church; W. E.
Rogers, layman of St. Paul; Charles Evan Holt, layman of
Duluth; F. H. Mellen, layman of Minneapolis; Henry Haggard
of Excelsior.

Among the professors and teachers named, besides Frank
H. Marshall, we find W. J. Lhamon and Carey E. Morgan,
ministers of the Portland Avenue Church, Minneapolis; Mary
Clipfell, later Mrs. H. A. Lemon; Sophia S. Holt, afterward
a missionary and leading church woman of Duluth; William
H. Reeves, Ernest Thornquist and during the last few months
of the college, Dan W. Morehouse is named both as student
and instructor. He was then of Watertown, South Dakota,
and afterward known to us as the brilliant president of
Drake University and masterly exponent of Astronomy.

As we read the list of students we notice well-known family
names of Minnesota and South Dakota. Myrtle and Percy
Leach of Aberdeen, South Dakota; several of the Chilton
family of Howard Lake, Luella McCaleb of Marion, Louida
Pew, Garden City, doubtless some connection of W. W. Pew,
the Sherwood family of Concord, Burdette Latham of Howard
Lake, several of the Haggard family whose address is given
as Fairpoint, Minnesota; Ella Buckles, Nettie Pew, John Karl

Osgood, Winifred Mills and J. Beebe, all listed as of Garden City; members of the Wray family of Concord, and Alfred F. Winship of St. Paul.

In the last prospectus, 1896-1897, the Departments of Instruction are given as The Bible, Philosophy and Civics, English Literature, Ancient Languages, Modern Languages, Mathematics, Natural Science, Instrumental Music, Elocution and Art. There was also a Commercial Department, a Normal Department and an Academic Department for students not prepared to take the college courses. What a pity such a college had to be discontinued!

It is evident that many students were helped to obtain part-time employment in Excelsior, which must always have been one of the fine playgrounds of Minnetonka.

In 1894-1895 the Faculty evidently was composed of eleven persons. Two of them held the degree of A.M., one an A.M., and Ph.D., three A.B., one M.D. and there were three instructors in Art, Commercial and Music departments. The year started without a president, but later there was called Albert Buxton, A.M. (Harvard) who was president when the work of the college ceased.

In the 1895 catalogue the following interesting item is found:

Tuition in College, per year	$ 28.00
Room rent and Board, 38 weeks (fuel and light extra)	76.00
Books—from $3 to $10 average	5.00
	$ 109.00

Another note advises that students may obtain room and board in private families for $3.00 a week. Maximum resident expenses for one college year, with fuel and lights, are estimated at $135 for "persons who practice rigid economy." In the same setting comes the statement, "parents or guardians wishing the faculty to exercise an oversight of the expenses of the students, should send the money direct to the president of the College, who will apply it as directed, and furnish an itemized account of such expenditures." Were these the good old days?

They were very courtly in those days, also. We read, in an item headed CO-EDUCATION: "Ladies are admitted to the same classes as gentlemen, and upon the same conditions.

The same labor is required of them as of men, and the same degree will be conferred at graduation. This system has been adopted upon the thorough belief in the ability of young women to stand side by side with young men in intellectual pursuits, and also in the mutually refining influence exercised in their associating together in schoolwork." This article was written almost thirty years before women were allowed to vote.

During the Christmas vacation, in 1896, the building was totally lost by fire. Students and faculty had made their in-influence felt in Excelsior's civic life. They were known for their courage in taking right attitudes on the liquor question. Their continuing would have meant much to the beautiful little town on Minnetonka. Yet, as I write, I know there have been years of carry-over of this short life of the North-western Christian College and that, through the lives of those who lived within its gates, its blessings extend even until now.

Is Another Educational Door About to Open?

This was the question when in 1911 Parker College, in Winne-bago, was offered for sale. Ministers, laymen and women made their way to this southern Minnesota town in September of that year to advise with the Baptist people who had operated the college for many years.

Some younger and less experienced people thought that by evening some agreement might be reached and that we and the Baptist committee would have dinner together, celebrating the first step taken toward another Christian College.

Disappointment came when we found the buildings in a run-down condition. The atmosphere was depressing. Many thought a southern Minnesota location would be too near Drake University. Those who knew Northwestern College compared the beauty of Excelsior with Winnebago, to the detriment of the latter. S. M. Waters and H. D. Kitson of Minneapolis were our chief spokesmen, as the findings of our deliberations were sent to the Baptist group, whose committee was in an adjacent room. Mr. Kitson was much interested in higher Christian education. He was a graduate of Hiram College and at that time a student at the University of Minne-sota. He was afterward a leading psychologist and a Pro-fessor at the University of Indiana.

—*Courtesy Mrs. A. G. Jenks.*

A. J. Buxton, first president of Northwestern Christian College, Excelsior, Minn.

A. B. Council of Northwestern Christian College, Excelsior. He attended the Mankato Convention, August 26, 1898.

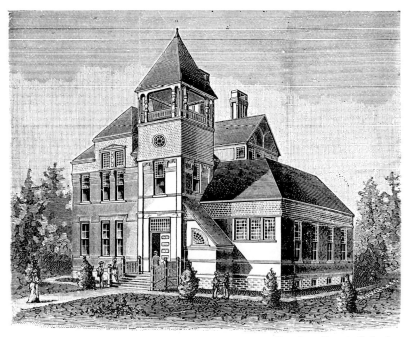

—*Courtesy Mrs. A. G. Jenks.*

Northwestern Christian College Building, Excelsior, Minn., 1891-1896.

Negotiations bogged down entirely. One of the number said: "Go back to the Baptist committee and say something that will close all this and mean no commitments." Late that evening, dinnerless and tired, we went home. Nothing further ever happened.

Thinking of the fine beginning made in higher Christian education before the turn of the century, one cannot but wonder what Minnesota churches might have been today had Northwestern Christian College continued, and had such men as Frank H. Marshall given their illustrious years in education to the North Star State. Should there have been faith enough to go on in 1896, or even 1911? Your historian has wondered if, with our beautiful location at Tipi Wakan, there might yet be an extension of one of our great Christian universities. New days do dawn. Perhaps some other historian may write of this years hence.

The Minnesota Christian Missionary Society

While we find stories of heroic evangelism in Minnesota from 1862, with mention of preaching as far back as 1855, the time of incorporation of the Minnesota Christian Missionary Society was in 1877. Business headquarters were Mankato. E. T. C. Bennett seems to have been president at the time of incorporation. His term of office is mentioned as 1875-1878.

Six years later we find that Leander Lane became Corresponding Secretary and Evangelist. The record notes that he held this office for ten years, except for one year—1890-1891, when he was pastor in Duluth. In that year, October 2, 1890, the articles of incorporation were changed at the State Convention in Duluth, making Minneapolis the place of business for the Minnesota Christian Missionary Society. Since the State for many years had a "delegate convention," it may have been these articles which instituted that plan. The articles were filed October 16, 1890.

When the United Christian Missionary Society was organized, the Minnesota Christian Missionary Society and the Christian Woman's Board of Missions in Minnesota wished to become one Board, patterned after the United Christian Missionary Society. By vote of the State Convention in 1921 the Articles of Incorporation of the Minnesota Christian Missionary Society were changed to include the work of the Christian Woman's Board of Missions, the two State Boards becoming one. The Articles called for the directorship to be composed of equal numbers of men and women. This plan of work was followed until 1944. These articles did not provide for a delegate convention. As the writer remembers, the delegate convention articles were changed by vote of the convention about 1918. However, this whole new Constitution or any intervening changes in Articles were never filed, though the plan of work was duly followed.

On July 3, 1926, the State Convention adopted the Articles under which it had been operating since 1921. These articles were signed by C. C. Crouch, president of the Minnesota Christian Missionary Society and Ada L. Forster, secretary, and filed on January 15, 1927. At that time the legal work for the society was being done by J. R. Everett, attorney, who so freely gave his services to the Society, as he does to this day.

Another change in Articles was made September 26, 1944, at the State Convention in St. Paul. The State Women's work was, by request, dropped from the Minnesota Christian Missionary Society. Otherwise no change in the plan of work was made. Signing the amended articles were C. C. McCaw, president, and Ada L. Forster, secretary. The missionary work of the women resumed the Constitution used by all State societies under the Department of Missionary Organizations of the United Christian Missionary Society. Mrs. L. Madge Smith of St. Paul was elected president. In September, 1950, at the State Convention held in St. Paul, First Church, further amendments in the Articles of Incorporation were presented to the Convention. These were acted upon in the 1951 Convention.

Among early evangelists were B. U. Watkins, V. M. Sandborn, David Overend, W. H. Burgess, David M. Haggard, Mr. and Mrs. J. A. Irwin, J. C. McReynolds and W. W. Pew, who is spoken of as "a deeply sacrificial minister of the circuit-riding order."

We will now, from records available, call the roll of those who have been officers and evangelists in Minnesota work.

Officers Minnesota Christian Missionary Society—

1875-1878	E. T. C. Bennett
1882	J. C. McReynolds
1883-1893	President, W. J. Lhamon, Minneapolis Secretary, Leander Lane served ten years as Corresponding Secretary and Evangelist except 1 year—pastor Duluth 1890-1891. Treasurer, A. E. Major, Howard Lake
1894-1895	President, W. J. Donaldson, St. Paul Treasurer, S. B. Robertson, Minneapolis Corresponding Secretary, F. H. Mellen, Minneapolis
1896-1899	President, Dr. David Owen Thomas, Minneapolis Treasurer, M. R. Waters, Minneapolis Corresponding Secretary, F. H. Mellen, Minneapolis

About 1896-1897 there evidently was a time of great evange-
lism in the State. The Christian Woman's Board of Missions
gave an appropriation for this project. Six men were at work.
They were Vernon J. Rose and E. W. Kerr (together), J. M.
Elam and T. A. Meredith (together), and Roy Caldwell and
C. M. Wickham (together).

1900-1903   President, A. D. Harmon, St. Paul

1902   Corresponding Secretary, J. K. Shellenberger,
            Madelia

1903   Corresponding Secretary, E. T. Gadd, St. Paul

1904   President, F. H. Mellen, Minneapolis
            Treasurer, Charles Oliver, Minneapolis
            Corresponding Secretary and Evangelist, J.
            H. Bicknell

1905   President, R. W. Abberly, Minneapolis
            Treasurer, Charles Oliver, Minneapolis
            Corresponding Secretary, M. R. Waters, Minne-
            apolis.

1905-1909   J. H. Bicknell, pastor of Central Church, St.
            Paul, also carried office of State Secretary,
            for the same period
            A. D. Harmon, minister of the First Church
            in St. Paul, was President.

1910-1912   There was a period when there was no State
            Secretary or Evangelist. For one year, 1911-
            1912, Ada L. Forster gave some time as pastor-
            at-large for the Minnesota Christian Missionary
            Society, giving special attention to churches
            which had part-time preaching.

1912   The state convention called C. B. Osgood to
            be Secretary-Evangelist for Minnesota. He
            remained in this position until 1918, when he
            became Regional Secretary of the north region
            including Minnesota, North and South Dakota.

1918   In the fall of 1918, Ada L. Forster, who had
            been leading in the work of Christian Woman's
            Board of Missions, became second Regional
            Secretary of the same area.

1920-1928   Mr. Osgood remained as regional secretary
            until 1920, when M. M. Moss became secretary

of the Minnesota Christian Missionary Society and also regional secretary. Mr. Osgood then gave his full time to South Dakota as evangelist, in which position he remained until 1928. He retained his headquarters in Minneapolis. Mr. Moss left the State in 1923 at which time Ada L. Forster became the only secretary in the north region of Minnesota and the Dakotas. This relationship lasted until 1928.

1928-1929 From 1928 to 1929 C. B. Osgood gave up his evangelism in South Dakota and became regional secretary once more. In the fall of 1929 the regional work ceased. During all the period the regional plan was only that of secretarial and evangelistic service. Each state had its own Board and Convention.

Those leading the State as presidents from 1912 were Ray E. Hunt, S. Grundy Fisher, Charles Oliver (layman) and C. C. Crouch (layman). The latter was president from 1920 to 1929. He was succeeded by George O.

1930-1952 Marsh. From the time of Mr. Marsh the president was the executive officer until the coming of Vernon S. Stagner in 1942. Others serving as presidents to that date were J. S. Leavitt, Arthur Poll, Max Deweese and Forrest L. Richeson. Mr. Stagner was called as secretary-evangelist in 1942 and he continues in that position to this time. Serving with him as presidents during that time are Forrest L. Richeson, C. C. McCaw, Clyde Leeds, and this year C. W. Hautzenrader.

Since 1910 several evangelists have served the State, for short periods, in a most acceptable manner. Among these are A. J. Hollingsworth, John G. Olmsted, Arthur Long, Hugh Cooper, Burton L. Huffman, Homer J. Armstrong and Mr. and Mrs. Lowell C. McPherson, who remained in the State for more than three years, giving notable service in all lines of church work.

Since January, 1949, the office of the State Society has been at the Protestant Center in Minneapolis. Interdenominational bodies of the State and also of the Twin Cities have offices in this building, as well as the State Societies of seven Communions. Board meetings of the occupants may be held at the Center. Chapel service each day is a means of bringing together all the workers in the building. The ecumenical spirit has been forwarded by this venture.

At the State Convention of 1950 the Regional Plan for Minnesota and the Dakotas was once more studied. Persons from these States were in the Convention. It was decided to submit the plan to the Boards of each State and the Minnesota Secretaries, Vernon S. Stagner and Mrs. C. W. Hautzenrader, were to visit churches in South Dakota. Thus the broader fellowship seemed, once more, on its way.

Many states have grown, in the same period of time, much greater in the number of churches than has Minnesota. Yet no one can estimate the value of the spiritual service by numbers. The work goes on with good courage by faithful servants, so we "thank God and take courage."

State Permanent Fund

Since soon after the close of the Northwestern College and the cessation of the Minnesota Christian Education Association, there has been a fund set aside under the above name. The Association must have ceased to function early in the twentieth century, since it was never mentioned in any convention that your historian remembers. We have always understood that the first money of this fund came from the sale of some lands owned by the Northwestern Christian College.

We have heard from Mr. M. R. Waters of the M. R. Waters and Sons Incorporated, (real estate and mortgage loans) of Minneapolis, the story of the first $3000.00 of the Permanent Fund. Mr. Waters found deeds to lands which the College owned. To quote his words as he said them to us: "The deeds were there, those preachers did not know they had anything of much value." Mr. Waters took the deeds to his office, watched for a good opportunity to sell the land and the above sum was the result. Thus the services of a layman were used for his church. Mr. Waters carefully invested the sum for the State Society. In this way the PERMANENT FUND of the Minnesota Christian Missionary Society had birth.

By the Constitution of the Minnesota Christian Missionary Society, money from bequests and sale of property coming to the Board was placed in this permanent fund.

Since the last year of the Northwestern Christian College is remembered as a hard financial year, there could have been no surplus from the College itself, but it has lived not only in the lives of its teachers and students, but in starting the permanent fund of Minnesota Missions.

In 1917, following the plan of many state organizations owning endowment funds, the Minnesota Christian Missionary Society, in convention assembled, voted that TRUSTEES OF THE PERMANENT FUND should be organized and incorporated, so making it unnecessary for the general treasury of the State Society to hold this fund with its current accounts. Thus the "Trustees of the Permanent Fund of the Minnesota Christian Missionary Society" came into being. Their Articles of Incorporation, dated May 29, 1918, authorize them to

receive from the Minnesota Christian Missionary Society all
moneys from bequests and sale of property legally belonging
to the Society, they in turn to invest the funds and to "pay to
the Society the interest on all such investments for use as the
Minnesota Christian Missionary Society shall decide." There
were to be FIVE TRUSTEES.

The said Trustees could, by their articles of incorporation,
fill vacancies in their number, the names of new trustees to be
brought before the annual convention of the Minnesota Christian Missionary Society for the endorsement of that body. The
five men elected at the time the new board was formed were:
Dr. George D. Haggard, R. T. Beebe, A. B. Leasure, S. M.
Waters, all of Minneapolis, and E. L. Sylvester of Plainview.
All these men were laymen and the practice of electing laymen has been followed to this day.

In 1919 when Tipi Wakan was acquired, the trustees of the
permanent fund were asked to hold the title to the property
for the State Society. The Minnesota Christian Missionary
Society has always done the business for Tipi Wakan and has
given an annual report to these trustees. The trustees were a
great help in the preparing of the BOND ISSUE at the time of
rebuilding Tipi Wakan. They held the fund accrued from the
insurance after the burning of the first Tipi Wakan building
until it was used for the new structure. As a long-time member of the state board, and former executive secretary, the
writer can pay tribute to the fine business sense, as well as the
helpful Christian spirit, of these trustees. Their investments
have been conservative and safe and there has never been any
loss from these investments.

At the present time the permanent fund is more than
$9,300.00.

The articles of incorporation of these trustees were recently
amended making the number of trustees to be not less than
five or more than seven. The trustees at this time (1950) are
A. N. Terry, Dr. George D. Haggard, Harold Jenkins, J. R.
Everett, A. R. Fowler and J. S. Leavitt.

The Christian Woman's Board of Missions

There can be no doubt that the pioneer women of Minnesota were thinking of Christian missions in a world-wide way even before the organization of the Christian Woman's Board of Missions in 1874, in Cincinnati, Ohio. We know they rejoiced greatly when this was acomplished.

In 1880 Mrs. A. P. Frost presided over the organization of the Minnesota Christian Woman's Board of Missions, during the State Convention at Pleasant Grove. She became its first president. We do not know who the other officers were, but from records and conversations we find among those intensely interested Mrs. John Truax, Mrs. T. T. Van Dolah, Mrs. D. N. Holmes, Miss Antoinette Chote, Mrs. E. T. Gadd, Mrs. B. H. Morgan, Mrs. Carey E. Morgan, Mrs. W. O. King, Mrs. Enos Campbell, Mrs. Love A. Sandborn, Mrs. Rebecca Faddis, Mrs. F. M. Parkinson, Mrs. Persis Nickum and Mrs. T. F. Mills. There must have been many others. Mrs. Enos Campbell organized the Missionary Society and Mission Band of the Portland Avenue Church in 1887.

As we first remember the women's missionary work, in 1907, Mrs. A. E. Major was acting as State Organizer. She served without salary and went to the churches as she was called. Among State Board members at that time were Mrs. A. D. Harmon, Mrs. Charles Oliver, who was president, Miss Florence Pierce, Secretary, Mrs. Perry J. Rice and Mrs. Alla M. Forster. Mrs. Major led almost all the churches to organize the woman's missionary society, she also had under her care a number of Mission Bands and many babies belonging to the "Little Light Bearers." The Missionary Intelligencer, the Missionary Tidings and Junior Buildings were to be found in every church.

From 1910 to 1920 presidents of the State organization were Mrs. Charles Oliver, Mrs. J. T. Ingersoll, Mrs. C. L. Kerr and Mrs. L. Madge Smith.

About 1909 the Twin City Union of women's missionary societies was organized. It was a strong organization, having three meetings each year and intervening board meetings. Many missionary projects cleared through this Union.

At this time, too, the Minnesota Summer School of Missions, an interdenominational fellowship, came into being. To this day our women have held offices in this work and taken part in all sessions of the annual school, though its name and leadership have changed with the years. Also our women have been given large responsibility in City and State Church Women's Councils as these have developed through the years.

In the days of District Conventions a period was set aside for the women's missionary work. There were district secretaries, who also served on the women's State Board. We recall the names of Mrs. C. M. Benham, Miss Marian Winship, Mrs. Sarah Hanley, Mrs. J. C. Hall, Mrs. Elizabeth Everett, Mrs. William Shoemaker, Mrs. George Koelsch, Mrs. C. S. White, Miss Ruth Mills, Reverend Edna M. Fellows, Mrs. A. J. Nightingale, Mrs. R. G. Mace, Mrs. Lee Rickey, Mrs. Ross Wray, Mrs. J. R. Everett, Mrs. Felix Jarboe, and Mrs. Martin Minor.

Regular secretaryship for Minnesota started with the part-time work of Ada L. Forster in 1911. With the development of the North-Central Region, comprising Minnesota, the Dakotas and Wisconsin, this became a full-time work. In 1928 Miss Mary White of Nebraska also looked after Minnesota and the Dakotas. When Minnesota again worked alone those serving as secretaries were Mrs. George O. Marsh, Mrs. J. S. Leavitt and Mrs. L. Madge Smith. Mrs. C. W. Hautzenrader is the present secretary. Since October, 1950, she once more has the regional task, Minnesota and the Dakotas.

The year 1920 saw many strong women's societies raising larger amounts than in former days. There were Mission Bands, Girls' Circles and Junior Missionary Societies. In all great movements of our church these societies did their full part; the Men and Millions Movement, the Golden Jubilee of the Christian Woman's Board of Missions when Minnesota raised $3,000 for a bungalow in India, war emergency drives and all other great challenges.

As the "independent" movement grew in the churches many societies withdrew. Those remaining today are as devoted as ever. In 1950 all of them had either met or were near to meeting their "Crusade" goals.

From 1920 to 1944 the State Christian Woman's Board of Missions worked as part of the Minnesota Christian Missionary Society. In 1944 the transfer was made back again to Minnesota Woman's Christian Missionary Society, following the constitution of the Missionary Organizations Department of the United Christian Missionary Society, with Mrs. L. Madge Smith as president.

Partly through the State Woman's Missionary Society, the Portland Avenue Society was challenged to become a "Living Link." On woman's day in the 1920 State Convention the state secretary said of the officers of that society: "Dare you telegraph headquarters asking to have Mary Campbell assigned to your church as missionary?" Miss Campbell had been a member of the Garden City, Minnesota, church and she was under appointment for India. They telegraphed and on that very day received the answer: "Miss Campbell assigned to Portland Avenue Woman's Missionary Society as Living Link."

That church, always a leader in missionary giving, has been a living link church ever since. Mrs. S. E. Arnold was president of the Portland Avenue society in 1920.

Though the societies today are fewer in numbers they are great in membership, devotion and stewardship. The annual gifts are even larger than in the days when there were more societies. We believe that in churches which have become independent there are women who long to enjoy the missionary society as they did in former years. Some of these keep in touch with the state conventions and give their personal offerings through the women's state board.

In the 1950 Convention the state women's board became the Minnesota Christian Women's Fellowship and the local societies were following in the same path. Mrs. W. K. Evans of the Sterling Church, Austin, is president.

Minnesota State Convention

In "Historic Personalities of Minnesota History" we find something of the importance of the "State Meeting," as they called it. We will let Mrs. T. T. Van Dolah speak. In a letter written to Charles B. Osgood, May 27, 1913, we read: "I know of yearly meetings in '59, '60, '61, '62. Again, I wrote you [former letter] only the cold facts about the early work and although you might read between the lines, hardships, self-denials, and pinching want both the worker and his family; you could never imagine the compensation in brotherly love and dear fellowship of the brethren; of the many and dear homes and their always loving welcome, giving freely, always, the best in material comforts and heart's affections to the evangelist and his wife; nor of the trust and faith each had in the other.

"Brother Osgood, these are priceless gifts. Fruits of God's love so far outweigh the hardships and trials and the lack of means, that their lingering sweetness is with us and will ever be with us, while the others are forgotten except as we find them recorded in some old diary or memorandum."

From an old photograph of pioneer preachers we find that they evidently had no trouble about the name of their convention. We find the words—"Disciples of Christ, Church of Christ and Christian Church." The convention held in Mankato, 1898, carries the footnote "Minnesota, 1856-1898."

It would seem, then, that the Minnesota Convention should hold its Centennial in 1956.

It is evident that the conventions were held in the churches to the year 1913. That year Ray E. Hunt and others conceived the idea of having week-long conventions of the outdoor type. In 1913 the convention was held at Antler's Park, a ground situated on a lake near Savage, about 30 miles from Minneapolis. Some folk lived in cottages, others in tents. A tent was the auditorium. Those living in cottages had to cross the lake in boats to attend each meeting. The cottages abounded in spiders. I remember counting 18 hiding in my hat one morning. Electric storms, much rain, mosquitoes, etc., took the joy out of life. Mr. and Mrs. Herbert Smith of Africa had to be doctored with quinine to save them from malaria. Yet, all in all, it was a great convention in fellowship and planning.

The outdoor convention would not be set aside, even though there was no entertainment available except as each person paid his own. From 1914 to 1919 we occupied the Baptist Camp ground at Mound, Minnesota, a place comfortable with cottages, auditorium and good dining hall. Many cooked meals in their cottages. So we came to have seven great days of fellowship, almost like the early conventions. Our speakers from abroad became family folk with us. J. H. Goldner, in 1926, said, "The Minnesota Convention is unique, just one big family. I know of nothing quite like it." Conventions on this plan continued in our own building, Tipi Wakan, from 1920 to 1941.

But all good things can wear out. About 1942 we again took our convention to the churches, making the length of time one evening and two whole days. Since this time the conventions have grown larger year by year.

Since about 1923 the "independent" influence has grown stronger in the State. Leaders strove to keep everyone represented on the programs and on committees and to keep the churches together in plans for constant growth through evangelism. Many fine contributions came from those who called themselves "independent," as well as others. Both the Minnesota Bible College and Drake University were represented in programs on Higher Christian Education. No one studying the trend of the conventions can doubt the sincerity of the state leaders in their desire to make the gatherings representative of all the churches of Minnesota. We regret to say that some churches are now never represented in the state conventions. Men of great minds have come to our conventions as "guest speakers," among them Joseph Chilton, Peter Ainslee, Jacob Goldner, and P. H. Welshimer. Dr. Edgar DeWitt Jones was the speaker in the 1950 convention.

For many years the convention has had fellowship with the Baptist Communion. At this time even closer connections are being sought. As in other states, societies representing social betterment in Minnesota are always welcome.

All the churches cooperating with our state and national boards have come to feel that the convention is their concern and that they must be represented and vocal in all its sessions.

As your historian studies the conventions from their beginning until now she cannot help but utter a fervent prayer that the wonderful unity of spirit known by the pioneers, and for many years afterward in planning evangelism in Minnesota, may yet come back to our churches. Surely there can be diversity of opinion but oneness in Christ. If the churches of the State today should all be represented in our conventions, we would need to go to an auditorium as no church would be large enough to hold us. As you read will you pray for a way to unity in the state we all love?

MINNESOTA DISTRICTS

While district conventions were held in Minnesota for many years the heyday of the District came in the days of the secretaryship of C. B. Osgood and Ada L. Forster, from 1913 to the early twenties. The districts were well defined, being Twin City, comprising Minneapolis and St. Paul churches, as well as those within about 50 miles of either city; the Southwest District, churches of Blue Earth, Le Sueur, Redwood, Martin, Watonwan, Nobles and Yellow Medicine counties; the Southeast District, churches of Dodge, Mower, Olmstead, Rice, Wabasha and Winona counties and the North District, including Aitken, Benton, Hubbard, Itasca, Polk, St. Louis and Todd counties. At one time the Duluth, Cohasset and Tamarack counties were called the Duluth District, meeting in their own convention.

The districts had their annual conventions, usually in the fall. Their officers planned their programs with the State Office. All phases of work were represented by the teams invited. These teams consisted of State Secretary, Missionary Secretary, representatives of Church School work and Young People's work. Usually there was 100% attendance of the churches of each district. Each district made its annual plan of work which usually included visitation among the churches and frequently the help of some new church. Some of the churches of the North District were founded in these days. In all districts there was great enthusiasm.

It was the "independent" spirit which broke the Districts away from the State Office in the middle twenties, especially in the Southeast and Southwest. The latter district organized churches in the following counties, after they became independent of other districts: Lyon County, Tracy Church;

Nicollet County, St. Peter Church; Pipestone County, Pipestone Church. The former district organized in Goodhue County, the Cannon Falls Church. However, State officers, evangelists and District officers did give service in these churches, especially early in their organization.

The Twin City District, including Hennepin, Ramsey, Wright, Stearns and Washington counties in early days, gradually shrunk to Minneapolis and St. Paul churches, but included Forest Lake and White Bear also. Other churches worked with the North District. Under the leadership, chiefly, of the St. Paul First Church, White Bear Lake Church was organized in 1943. Until recently an annual function of the Twin City District was the Brotherhood Dinner. This became a great event in program, attendance and offering.

The Twin City Union, an organization of the Women's Missionary Societies since about 1910, still holds evening meetings three times a year. These are general church meetings.

Minnesota is a large state. We can conclude that the District plan has its own carry-over to this day and that, independent or otherwise, churches have been and still may be founded and strengthened by the fellowship of the congregations that can easily reach each other.

SCATTERED DISCIPLES

A strange name perhaps, but the body of people so designated meant much to Minnesota Missions, and the State work and workers to them. It was after the coming of C. B. Osgood to the work in 1912, that Disciples who lived in towns in which we did not have a church were sought out. From that time to about 1930 secretaries and evangelists considered themselves pastors-at-large to these people.

There were many names on this list, from all sections of Minnesota. These received state and district convention programs from the state office, they were encouraged to subscribe for the state paper and it was suggested to them that they give, not only to state missions, but to the national missionary boards of the church.

When there were several families in a town, state workers visited them. While it was never suggested to them that they do other than work in some local church, there were occasions when they did make plans to get together at intervals. They were urged to receive the Lord's Supper together. When the towns in which any of these folk lived were in the line of travel, state workers made many a welcome visit. It was always left to the people themselves to decide if an attempt should be made to organize a church in their town.

We can think of a number of families who gave regularly and largely to our state and national missions. They became very dear friends and they were almost always in our conventions. One of these, Nimrod Victor, was a member of our State Board for many years. He and Mrs. Victor afterward had the joy of moving to Minneapolis and serving in the Portland Avenue Church. The Featherstone family, of Red Wing, were great and interested folk, as were many others.

All in all, we were blessed by knowing these "Scattered Disciples." Most of them took national papers and missionary magazines and rejoiced in their Christian Church background and teaching. Some of them saw to it that their children had opportunity to make Confession of Faith and receive baptism in their own church. There must have been over two hundred names of such Disciples on record.

The State Paper

Looking over old records we find that the first mentioned State paper is *The Christian Gleaner.* We note a quotation from it in 1891 and we would presume it was, at that time, a well-established paper.

In the State Convention of 1897 there is mention of "Our Northwestern paper, *The Christians News;* W. W. Greenwood, Minneapolis, Editor."

It is probable, after the turn of the century, that *The Minnesota Christian* came to be the organ of the Minnesota Christian Missionary Society. The State Evangelist was C. R. Neal. The pastor of the Central Christian Church, St. Paul, J. H. Bicknell, was also state secretary and editor of the paper about 1906.

At almost every convention, State and District, much was said about the cost of the paper to the State Board. Sometimes there would be talk of abandoning it, but always its service in development of the State program weighed largely to offset all it cost.

Editors, too, were hard to find. When there was an executive secretary it was his work to edit the State paper. When no such officer existed some minister, with a few exceptions, became editor. We remember, before 1918, editors were Mona Leavens, office secretary of the Minnesota Christian Missionary Society, W. H. Knotts, minister, Richard Dobson, minister, and C. B. Osgood, State Secretary.

After the Regional plan came in 1918 *The Minnesota Christian* became the *Northern Christian.* It served the churches of North and South Dakota and Minnesota. Since that time, with two exceptions, state or regional secretaries have been editors.

However, with the discontinuance of the region in 1929, the *Northern Christian* was once more a Minnesota organ. Editors from 1918 to date have been C. B. Osgood, M. M. Moss, Ada L. Forster, Anna Kramer of St. Paul, Mardelle Jackson of Minneapolis and Vernon S. Stagner, the present editor.

May the *Northern Christian* continue its work of Christian Fellowship!

The Story of Tipi Wakan

(The Lodge of the Great Spirit)

October 31, 1919, marked one of the great movements of Minnesota church history. On that rainy night more than a hundred persons braved the weather and drove to Woolnough, Inn, on Lake Minnetonka, to take over the property which was to become Tipi Wakan. This night marked the realization of the spiritual dream of Mildreth J. Haggard, her dream of years for the young people of Minnesota. When she, with Ada L. Forster, L. A. Brumbaugh, and J. S. Leavitt began the young people's conference movement in Minnesota, in a small conference at Portland Avenue Church in Minneapolis, January 1919, mention was made of her hope to find some place that the Disciples of Christ in Minnesota might purchase, preferably on Lake Minnetonka. At that time the Baptists and Methodists owned such camp grounds on the lake. During the summer of 1919 Miss Haggard was on Lake Minnetonka in the steamboat "Victor" with Captain George Hopkins, the well-known figure of the Minnetonka steamer days, when he pointed out the Woolnough Inn and mentioned that it was for sale. With more than five and a half acres and a well-appointed three-story building, with central heat and a caretaker's apartment, it would have seemed to some people too big a project, but not to as brave a person as Mildreth Haggard. She found the price to be about $7000.00. During the war such property had done very little business. Steps were taken at once to interest others. From the first, Tipi Wakan was thought of as a place to be shared with other Christian communions for their conferences and conventions. So summer and early fall of 1919 led to the opening of the house on this Halloween evening, with a well-prepared dinner and program of dedication.

As always, the work of financing was done by a few leaders. The down payment was to be made November 1. We did not have the money ready on October 31 and early the next day teams went out to collect the sum needed. Dr. George D. Haggard and Miss Mildreth made the first gifts. Many liberal sums were donated, as well as linens and extra furnishings.

Tipi Wakan

The summer of 1920 found us holding the first Young People's conference in our new home. We might add here that Oklahoma and Minnesota were the only states to hold conferences in 1919. Leaders from these states at once gave service in setting up the conference movement for our Brotherhood. Our 1920 conference was attended by persons from Winnipeg, Canada, Iowa, South Dakota, Wisconsin and Illinois. It was a great beginning for "TIPI WAKAN ON THE LAKE SO BLUE." For several years Wisconsin, the Dakotas and Iowa young people made Tipi Wakan their conference. Our State Convention also met at Tipi Wakan.

M. M. Moss, at that time secretary of Minnesota missions, prepared an attractive Tipi Wakan folder which went to many states. In order to keep the house open all summer some folk, chiefly from the Twin Cities, formed the Tipi Wakan Club to which they paid dues. Mr. and Mrs. Johnny Reid, of Minneapolis were in charge of the house. Many persons from Minnesota and other states had their vacations that year in this fine spot. However, after the first year, the Club was discontinued and Tipi Wakan was used for Christian education only.

We should say something about the building of those days. On the first floor we had a beautiful hall, with fireplace; dining room, overlooking the lake, also with a fireplace; as fine a dining room as one would find in any first-class hotel. What had been a dance hall in hotel days was our assembly hall. These rooms face the lake as did also a large porch, screened, furnished with plenty of easy chairs, and always filled with appreciative guests. Kitchens and storerooms were also on the first floor. On the southside lower floor was a nice apartment which could be occupied by a caretaker. On the second and third floors were bedrooms, and each floor had a central room which was used as a sitting room. The second floor also had a screened porch. Mr. L. O. Pettit was one of the leaders of the Tipi Wakan Club and he acted as a manager for a time. Mrs. Alvina Reid remained as the head of the house during all the time that we were in the first building. After the ruling by the Minnesota Christian Missionary Society that Tipi Wakan should be used for religious education and church-related work for ourselves and other religious groups, the property became tax free. Any money over and above the general expenses was applied on the payments for the building.

The year 1925 found us with the property clear of debt. Our Young People's conference that year was a great one and the largest State Convention held at Tipi Wakan was also in that year. By September we had taken our yearly inventory and left the house closed, with a caretaker in the apartment. The writer, then State Secretary for Minnesota, was just leaving the office when Robert Newton, pastor of the Portland Avenue Church, called to say that Tipi Wakan was burning. A sad company of folk assembled on the hill, the spot where so many young folk had known high spiritual experiences, and there watched everything that had been acquired burn to the ground. There was little wind and because of that the pagodas and the beautiful boathouse built in 1923-1924 were not burned. We should say that the property had been much improved during the five years and the loss was a tragedy.

In 1926 the Young People's conference and the State Convention were held at Mound, Lake Minnetonka, then Baptist property. There were fine gatherings in attendance and program. Just about everyone visited our "ruins." Some of us ate supper there one evening. Seated on green spots closest to the building, we prayed there that we might meet in our own building in 1927, and we did. Jacob E. Goldner of Cleveland, Ohio, was our guest speaker at the convention of 1926, and he was much interested in our rebuilding Tipi Wakan, as were many national leaders who had come to love our home. F. E. Smith, then leader of our Ministerial Relief and Pension Board, said that we did not dare to let the place go, as it was too important that we keep it. Many board meetings were held in 1926-1927. Some of the trustees of the permanent funds, who held the deed to the property, by consent of the Director of the Minnesota Christian Missionary Society, suggested putting the $9000.00 that remained from insurance into some investment, the interest of which might be used for Christian education, thus financing a place in which the Young People's conference could be held each year.

The majority of Minnesota people favored rebuilding. Other communions who by that time had made Tipi Wakan their conference home also hoped that we would carry on.

The matter of financing a new building was investigated. We found that the sum necessary would be more than $14.000 at least. C. C. Crouch was president of the State Society and Ada L. Forster, Secretary. They suggested the sale of bonds up to $6000. J. R. Everett, attorney, and a group of businessmen, as well as the trustees of the permanent funds, promptly made ready the bond issue for sale. The bonds were sold through the State office. They were to draw 6% interest and were payable in ten years. There was no difficulty in selling them. Housewives, elderly folk and business people soon saw the opportunity of investing in so interesting a project. There was no expense for the sale of the bonds and something over $15,000.00 was on hand for the new structure early in 1927, at which time bids were received from several contractors.

Those closest to the hard task knew many discouragements. The greatest hurdle was that there could be no beauty in the new structure for many a day. It had to be tar paper on the outside; basement dining room and kitchen, rooms of the plainest summer sort, small, unimposing hall, no porches, and all this difference loomed largely with many and led to suggested delays. The writer would not dare to mention names of the folk who wanted to go ahead, save the two who were closest to the task, C. C. Crouch, President of the State Board, and J. S. Leavitt of St. Paul, who had directed our conferences from 1920 to 1925. Mrs. B. F. Hazeltine of the Portland Avenue Church added an extra $500.00 to build what has been known through the years as the "boys' dorm." It was not until April, 1, 1927, that the contract was signed and the building commenced. We had to be ready by the middle of June for our Young People's conferences and the State Convention.

As the building progressed we found there would be no money left for furnishings. We asked Mr. E. M. Hanson to figure the cost of the furnishing of each room, including bedrooms, auditorium, dining rooms and kitchen. We then "sold" the bedrooms at $37.50 per room, the donors of that amount having a name plate on the room which they furnished. This gave no privileges save the privilege of helping to furnish our new home. Similarly, folk gave for the furnishing of the dining room, hall, as assembly room and kitchen. The entrance hall was made as "Indian" as it could be with our limited means. Mrs. Kate Everett, Miss Lorna Tuttle and members of the Laura Lynn Circle of the Portland Avenue Church did most of the work on the hall. Many persons also provided linens, curtains and dresser cloths for the rooms.

There was a last-minute rush to get ready for our Young People's conference which opened on a Monday evening. On the Saturday before that, about twenty-five people put the finishing touches to our Tipi Wakan, that the young people might be comfortable. Many men glued chairs together, since they came in separate parts from the factory, all worked until dark, thankful and yet sad, at the crude beginning we were obliged to make. Mrs. Alvina Reid, faithful as ever, was in charge. On that Saturday night the heaviest rains of the season came, flooding the basements of many houses. Our dining room was damp, our housekeeper and staff discouraged, but when Monday evening came and the young people trooped in, it was all gladness. They assured us that they were glad to have Tipi Wakan back again and said to those discouraged oldsters, "Just forget it, we'll all help, and watch us have a good time."

We had to build up our patrons once more. Some large conferences had found other places in 1926. We were obliged to limit the number we could take and for some time extended our guest list by using the second floor of the boathouse as a dormitory and also by using some tents.

Year by year, young people beautified the chapel. The motto put in our chapel bore the words "They Go From Strength to Strength." Surely we were comforted by it. As other conferences came to Tipi Wakan, they also donated little improvements to our home, which came to be beloved once more by them as well as by us. By 1933 the depression was upon us and many felt the load too great, some wanting to sell the building. As usual God had his Joshua to lead the people. The outside had never been finished. George O. Marsh, minister of the Portland Avenue Church, led the people in a drive to buy asbestos shingles with which the outside of the building was finished, found volunteers to nail them on and kept the Tipi Wakan spirit alive. From 1928 to 1935 the writer came yearly from her ministry in Milwaukee, Wisconsin, to visit Tipi Wakan, and never doubted that God meant us to retain this place in which so many young people had learned to find out their Father's will more completely. So the building remained through the depression, being improved each year. Porches were added at length and the second floor dormitory above the "boys' dorm." Meanwhile, interest had been paid each year on the bonds and about $2000.00 on the principal.

By 1940 when Forrest L. Richeson was chairman of the State Board, and Ada L. Forster, secretary, it seemed wise to re-finance Tipi Wakan. Four thousand dollars was borrowed from the Sons of Norway Insurance Company on a ten-year plan at 5½% interest. All the bondholders were paid, the depression had come and gone, NOT ONE PERSON LOST MONEY ON TIPI WAKAN.

It was at the time of this refinancing that we found out what other people thought of our property. When J. S. Leavitt took the representatives of the insurance company to see Tipi Wakan, the writer asked him if they liked the property, and he replied, "They were so delighted with it that they would not mind if we failed to pay the loan." We felt that our property, for thirteen years a problem, had become one of the firm foundations of Minnesota faith.

Forrest L. Richeson and Ada L. Forster cared for the business of Tipi Wakan until 1944. That year Vernon S. Stagner, then State Secretary of the Minnesota Christian Missionary Society, who had already become familiar with Tipi Wakan procedure, took over the business leadership.

Year by year a greater number of conferences and groups used Tipi Wakan and many improvements were made. We might add here that the place had always been self-supporting, even in the hardest years. On September 25, 1950, during the convention of the Minnesota Christian Missionary Society, held in St. Paul, First Church, the ceremony of burning the legal papers of the 1940 mortgage took place. Those officiating were C. W. Hautzenrader, president of the State Society, A. N. Terry, Chairman of the trustees of the permanent funds; J. R. Everett, also a trustee, and Ada L. Forster, who was visiting from California. It was an occasion for great rejoicing and the triumphant end of a long, hard, but glorious road.

The above event was not the only one for rejoicing. Under the splendid leadership of Vernon S. Stagner, a beautiful property adjacent to Tipi Wakan had been added. Known in former days as "Oliver Lodge," the summer home of Mr. and Mrs. Charles Oliver, it was bought by them in 1923, that it might not be used for purposes that would be detrimental to a Christian camp. We had often wished to add this property to that which we possessed. When once more the property was for sale at the sum of $16,500, the Minnesota Christian Missionary Society felt that it must be purchased. The new property gives us a spacious home and four additional acres of land, as well as a small cottage to be used by a caretaker. There is added space for 46 extra guests as well as room for help, modern kitchen, basement for dishwasher and storage, with service elevator. The beautiful porch has been made into a dining room and is sufficiently large for all guests. One room is used as a chapel.

By 1952 the indebtedness on the new property is $7500. To-day, Minnesota churches have a self-supporting property. Best of all, it is the Lodge of the Great Spirit to thousands of folk who have lingered there for these thirty summers.

The 1950 season closed with 2400 guests on the register, these representing eight Christian Communions and 50 Conferences, as well as Interdenominational and Educational Institutions.

As for our own use of Tipi Wakan we have grown from one Young People's conference in 1920, to at least six events each year, Young People's Conference, Chi Rho Camp, Men's, Women's, Business Women's and Family Conferences, as well as the State-wide Planning Conference of the Minnesota Christian Missionary Society. The 1950 Family Camp was of our own Church and the Baptist Communion together.

May "The Great Spirit" continue to give to many, in this spot we have dedicated to Him, glorious mornings, noons of Christian fellowship, peaceful evenings and nights of praise and rest.

The first buildings at Tipi Wakan on Lake Minnetonka.

Tipi Wakan as it was rebuilt following the fire.

The Minnesota Bible College

One cannot give the story of this educational institution without going back into the history of what was known sometime between 1880 and 1890 as the "Scandinavian Mission." We have also heard it called the "Swedish Mission." We have ascertained that this work was never incorporated.

At that time Julius Stone, minister of the Church of Christ, Chippewa Falls, Wisconsin, sought out W. J. Lhamon, minister of the Portland Avenue Church in Minneapolis. This led to a meeting with Robert Moffatt, of the American Christian Missionary Society, and one named as Brother Devold. It was an attempt to get the Society to help in starting a work among Scandinavians in Minneapolis. Since help was not given at that time, Mr. Devold remained and worked in Minneapolis at his own expense. Later, C. A. Holmgren was supported by the State Society and the American Christian Missionary Society, but in a short time the work was dropped. Still another attempt was made, the same Societies helping to support Charles Nelson. A meeting place was secured at this time, but the work did not thrive and it was discontinued.

In 1908 Mr. Stone met with M. R. Waters and Charles Oliver in Minneapolis. Mr. Stone had noticed the success of D. E. Olson, an evangelist, and he wished to secure him for work among the Scandinavian people. About 1910 Mr. Olson and Walter Burton held a meeting in Rochester. At that time, also, there was an opportunity to buy the Baptist Temple, at 23rd Street and Bloomington Avenue South in Minneapolis, a Scandinavian neighborhood.

Perhaps here we ought to describe David Eugene Olson. He was born in 1876, of Lutheran parents. He united with the Church of Christ in Port Townsend, Washington. He received his A.B. degree from the Eugene Bible University, Eugene, Oregon. Mr. Olson attracted attention. He was a man of strong physique. His rather long hair was red-gold and he wore a long-tailed coat and walked very swiftly; every move he made was that of an athlete. He could sing as well as preach, could engage in callisthenics, and we have heard it remarked that he could run from Genesis to Revelation in one breath.

Upon the coming of Mr. Olson in 1912, Julius Stone resigned his connection with the American Christian Missionary Society in order to clear the way for Mr. Olson to become leader of the new enterprise. So it came about that, in the spring of 1912, a meeting was held at the West Hotel in Minneapolis. Together with support promised to Mr. Olson by the American Christian Missionary Society and the Minnesota Christian Missionary Society and large individual gifts, which came mostly from the Portland Avenue and Grand Avenue churches in Minneapolis, the work was launched. C. S. Osterhus became a co-worker. Mr. Stone was always an interested helper.

Mr. Olson then toured in other states, describing the building we were to buy as "The Great White Temple." He also talked of the training of ministers as part of his project. Ultimately, with I. N. McCash in leadership, the coveted building was dedicated. Thereafter, in State and District Conventions, as well as in National Conventions, Mr. Olson gathered funds for the work. He raised much money. Had Mr. Olson been as good in business planning as he was in raising funds, the financial career of the Minnesota Bible College might have followed a less chequered road.

Eventually Mr. Osterhus and Mr. Olson separated, and in March 1913 Mr. Olson transferred his interest to a property on University and 15th Avenues, Southeast, a corner opposite the University of Minnesota campus, which he thought might belong to the University. He found that it was privately owned and that its cost was estimated at $25,000.

Mr. Olson always spoke of the acquiring of this land as almost a miracle. The owner considered the land worth the sum already named, but, to quote from information supplied by the Bible College, was told, "If you will agree to erect a Bible College, on it (the land) within five years, and will lay a $10,000 foundation within a year, we will give it to you for $12,000." This seems to have been on a 99-year lease.

It was about this time that Mr. Olson incorporated his work as "The Scandinavian Christian Missionary Society and International Bible Mission." It was his intention at that time to establish a number of Bible Colleges at strategic points in the United States.

Many of the pledges made at the West Hotel meeting in 1912 were on a five-year plan and were continued in behalf of the new location. Julius Stone, Victor Carter and Samuel Potts were fine helpers in business. The substantial basement of the present building was finished, according to the requirements, within the year.

There was at this time the University Place Christian Church, a project of the Minnesota Christian Missionary Society and the American Christian Missionary Society, whose chief leaders were Mr. and Mrs. E. S. Wood, former members of the Portland Avenue Church. A little company of folk, with some fine young students of the Minnesota University, were meeting in a house on 17th Avenue and 4th Street, Southeast. The downstairs had been made over as a chapel and the minister, Grover C. Schurman and family, resided on the upper floor. Mr. Olson connected himself with this church, which sold its property in behalf of the new college building, with the understanding that the church meet there, preserving its own autonomy as a church.

The mammoth task of finishing the building within the five years was followed, and the present beautiful structure was dedicated July 14, 1918. By this time, to the great regret of many who started with Mr. Olson, the College was "independent," thus breaking for the first time the beautiful spirit of unity which had existed in Minnesota from pioneer days.

The student body grew year by year. It was in 1919 that G. H. Cachiaras was added to the faculty. A graduate of Johnson Bible College and having studied at Drake University, he came as a teacher of Greek. He afterward received his M.A. degree from the University of Minnesota. He has the longest service of any member of the Bible College faculty and for many years he has acted as Dean, during which time he has been appreciated by faculty and students, as well as fellow workers of the Minnesota Christian Missionary Society.

Mr. Olson remained as president and business manager of the college until 1922. At that time the project was in debt and the property went into receivership. Mr. Olson consulted with his friend, President Eugene V. Sanderson of Eugene Bible University, Eugene, Oregon. Mr. Sanderson was also president of what was then known as the International Bible Mission.

Mr. Sanderson redeemed the property from receivership in July, 1924. College historians tell us that Mr. Olson raised $55,000 of the fund paid for this purpose. During Mr. Sanderson's leadership, which lasted until 1932, the college was known as the Minnesota Bible University and also as part of the International Bible Mission.

Following the depression years the college was hard pressed once more financially and Floyd Jones, a musician of note, became president. One of the high lights of his administration was the College Choral Club, members of which traveled under his auspices to churches, State and national conventions and thus made the college known to many people. Mr. Jones stayed until 1935. During that time the college was made solvent.

Another "Moses" came in the person of Paul A. Millard, who had spent many years as minister of the Worthington Church in Minnesota. Self-sacrificing teachers had allowed their salaries to get into arrears. Mr. Millard, while still retaining his ministry in Worthington, gave his service free of charge while raising $27,000 to pay the debt of the institution. He remained as president until 1944.

During Mr. Millard's administration he was bereft of his dear wife, Leah Walker Millard, a woman beloved and well known in Minnesota. The Leah Millard dormitory was dedicated to her memory.

In 1945 Russell E. Boatman undertook the presidency of the college which he holds to this date.

Quoting from the 1950-51 bulletin we find that the Minnesota Bible College "is accredited by:

"The Accrediting Association of Bible Colleges and Institutes (College Division). It is listed in the Current Bulletin of the United States Office of Education—'Accredited Higher Institutions.' Is approved by the State Department of Education for the training of veterans, under Public Laws 16 and 346, and the United States Department of Justice for the training of foreign students. Is chartered by the state of Minnesota as a non-profit theological college, with the privilege of awarding appropriate degrees and certificates."

The same bulletin gives the number of the student body as 211. The faculty listed are: Russell E. Boatman, B.Th., B.O., M.A., B.D., president; G. H. Cachiaras, A.B., M.A., B.D., D.D., dean; O. A. Trinkle, B.S., A.B., D.D.; Eulah Hall, M.S.S., Wichita Business College, B.S.L.; Edith Flick, B.S., Indiana State Teacher's College, M.S., with 35 years' teaching experience in public school; Manson E. Miller, A.B., M.A.; Ronald F. Keeler, B.S., State Teacher's College, Bloomsburg, Pa., A.B., M.A.; William Homer Sperry, A.B., M.A.; Conley D. Silsby, B.Th., B.O., A.B., M.A.; Don Earl Boatman, B.Th., A.M., B.D., M.Th.; Lawrence C. Sunkler, B.M, B.Th., A.M., B.D.; Mrs. Eunice Sunkler, B.M.; Pheraba Hoskins, A.B.; William Griffin, A.B., B.D., M.A.; William S. Phillips, B.S.

Faculty members with the longest service are: G. H. Cachiaras from 1919; Manson E. Miller, 1937; and Ronald F. Keeler, 1938 and William H. Sperry, 1940.

The gross value of the buildings is cited at $650,000. Besides the main college building there is Leverton Hall, a women's dormitory; Millard Hall, a men's dormitory; two apartment houses for married couples; president's home and a central heating plant. The college also owns Pine Haven Lodge on Long Lake near Park Rapids, Minnesota. This property is used for young people's conferences. Several acres of timber land on the shores of Long Lake have been given to the college by R. E. Farrand of Des Moines, Iowa. There is a proposed extension to the property to be erected on the side of Leverton Hall, which when finished will give fireproof residence and dining facilities for both men and women students, and a gymnasium.

The number of graduates to date is 444. Among those graduates are persons who either have worked or will work in several Foreign Mission Fields: Mr. and Mrs. Bernel E. Getter, India; Mr. and Mrs. Paul Nielsen, Japan; Mr. and Mrs. Melvin Huckins, Okinawa; Mr. and Mrs. Carl Fish, Okinawa; Mr. and Mrs. Mark G. Maxey, Japan; Mrs. Albert Esculto, Philippines; Mr. and Mrs. Benjamin F. Allison, Philippines; Mr. O. D. Johnson, India; Mr. and Mrs. Max Randall, South Africa; LaVerne Morse, Tibetan Border; and Mr. and Mrs. Kenneth Fox, Brazil.

Many students of the Bible College have served in Minnesota churches, and churches of other states. The professors also have regularly supplied pulpits. Arthur Poll, a graduate of the College, is minister of the University Place Church at this time. Graduates have gone to churches having small budgets. Having been in the homes of some of these men, we know that their sacrifice has frequently been great. We have also known some of the homes from which they went out to college; good, Christian homes which nurtured them in the "Faith of Our Fathers."

Some of these men have felt it right to oppose the organizations to which other lives had been devoted, and by and through which the early pioneers in Minnesota lived and served, as they let the "Restoration Plea" claim its place in the North Star State. Yet we believe that all of us have tried to exalt our Lord and Master and in this we have been together.

Should we not remember the greater price than ours paid by the pioneers in establishing, in the last half of the nineteenth century, the foundations upon which we have been building in the first half of the twentieth century?

THE CHURCHES

From a history compiled by Mrs. J. S. Leavitt in 1941, we gather most of the facts here recorded. Mrs. Leavitt has used some earlier histories in preparing her booklet.

In 1865, Mrs. Deborah Arbuckle came to St. Paul from Ohio. Finding no church of the Disciples of Christ, she placed her membership with the Baptist church. Two years later, Mr. and Mrs. W. A. Faddis came to the city from Le Sueur, Minnesota. Mr. Faddis was connected with a commercial college, and to this college A.M. Haggard, son of Elder David M. Haggard, came in 1872.

Mr. and Mrs. Edwin Stewart and three children came from England to St. Paul in 1874 and they were anxious for church privileges. That same year, in September, Elder J. C. McReynolds, State Evangelist, preached to the people, who met in the homes of the little group. S. C. Arbuckle, Jr., and a son of the Stewarts were baptized. Mrs. Arbuckle withdrew her Baptist affiliation and joined them. During this winter, Elder B. U. Watkins, another Minnesota evangelist, came to preach for them.

On March 15, 1873, the Disciples rented a small Unitarian chapel, for $100 a year; they were to use it during such periods as the Unitarians did not occupy it. Here Mr. Watkins preached. It is interesting to know that Father Ireland, a missionary of the Roman Catholic Church, and later Archbishop of the great St. Paul Cathedral, upon attacking Protestantism, drew a reply from Mr. Watkins, who was well able to defend his position. Every effort was made at this time to find other Disciples in the city. One, Hannah Biggs, of Lexington, Kentucky, who had lived six years in St. Paul, joined the group at the time, and others were added.

On Lord's Day, March 21, 1875, the first church organization was completed. W. A. Faddis was elected elder and S. C. Arbuckle, Jr., and Edwin Stewart as deacons. With them, charter members were: Laura Faddis, Deborah E. Arbuckle,

TWIN CITY CHURCHES

Harriet C. Stewart, Annie Wraith, Hargrave Wraith, John Wraith, Arthur H. Wilcox, Hannah Biggs, Miss Ballard, A. M. Haggard, C. S. Haggard, C. H. Pierce, Sarah Arbuckle and M. D. Alexander.

This church met regularly on the Lord's Day for worship and the Lord's Table, and on Thursdays for "prayer and exhortation." Occasionally a preaching brother came along and helped. One of these was James Vernon, Jr., of Kipton, Ohio, "who was with the brethren seven Lord's Days." He received into the church "Sister A. H. Wilson, Sister F. Roberts, and Brother S. C. Arbuckle, Sr."

The latter part of the same year, full possession of the building was obtained for $200 per year and Ira Chase, of Peoria, Illinois, preached over three Lord's Days. By this effort fifteen were added to the church. Appeals were printed and sent out to sister churches for help in securing a building, but with small result. About this time six charter members moved from the city, a great loss to the small church. However, cheer was brought by the arrival of B. U. Watkins, bringing a $100 gift for the church, and remaining with them for two Lord's Days. His teaching meant much to them.

The first Sunday school was organized in May, 1876, and the first session held May 21. F. D. Butler, a new member, was the first superintendent. His wife was a gifted woman and they added strength to the church, Mr. Butler sometimes preaching.

Preaching for short periods, at this time, were Ira J. Chase of Peoria, Illinois, Brother Dungan of Oskaloosa, Iowa, and N. J. Aylsworth of Fort Wayne, Indiana. The latter was called as part-time minister. Friends outside the church helped on the expense. Sister S. B. McLean of New York promised $100 and David Overend of Pleasant Grove, Minnesota, the same amount. Brother Pier of Mantonville, Minnesota, gave $50 and $150 was raised by the church. Mr. Aylesworth was succeeded, about May, 1877, by Brother John La Grange, who preached every other Lord's Day.

About October, 1877, the meeting place of the church was changed to the Gospel Temperance Club on Seventh Street, near Jackson. An interesting note reads: "A pulpit was built for any preacher who might happen along." Then a sad note: "Soon after this the church ceased to meet for a time,

TWIN CITY CHURCHES

stored their belongings and, for the time being, gave up the struggle." The latter note is of February, 1878.

In 1882, John Hay, minister of "the new church in Minneapolis" (Portland Avenue), preached to the people for several Lord's Days, in the afternoon. Through him, Leander Lane of Marshalltown, Iowa, became minister. The meeting place was a room in the Y. M. C. A. building. During this ministry the church was visited by Robert Moffet of the American Christian Missionary Society, by Enos Campbell of Minneapolis and F. D. Power of Washington City. There is mention that the General Missionary Board (American Christian Missionary Society) was a "never-failing friend of the St. Paul church," and the statement that without that Board the church might not have been in existence.

During the ministry of C. L. Brokaw, who followed Mr. Lane, a lot was purchased on Carroll Street, between Louis and Cathedral Place. A building was bought and moved to this location. The church spoke of themselves, at this time, as being "the happiest little church in existence." The congregation seemed, at this point, to feel sure of the future.

The next ministry, that of W. A. Foster of Brookville, Indiana, marked the purchase of the lot on which the church now stands, for $9,000. This was indeed a choice location of that day. The recently remodeled building from Carroll Avenue was placed on the rear of the lot. Following Mr. Foster, E. R. Edwards and A. R. Moore each had a pastorate of three years.

The ministry of A. D. Harmon, beginning in 1897 and continuing until 1911, saw the greatest growth yet known to the church. Mr. and Mrs. Harmon were graduates of Cotner College and people of great faith. Mrs. J. S. Leavitt's record says of them: 'His brilliant sermons and his warm, friendly personality brought into the church many people. He seldom had to provide a substitute for the pulpit, as Mrs. Harmon could preach a splendid sermon whenever needed. It was during this period that the church seemed to get her 'stride' and became a great power in the State."

The first six years of this ministry were spent in planning the building which we now know as First Church. It was a tremendous undertaking in a city a great part Roman Catholic.

TWIN CITY CHURCHES

Your historian has heard incidents of this struggle. One of them was that the Harmons grew discouraged when the building was proceeding. So great and many were the problems that Mr. Harmon faced them alone, at the partly finished structure, wondering if they could go on. Faith conquered. This man and woman saw their beautiful building finished and the family they were rearing become Henry G. Harmon, President of Drake University; Margueritte Harmon Bro, missionary, world traveler and writer; Harriet Harmon Dexter, Professor of English in Northland College, Ashland, Wisconsin, and leader in the National Council of Church Women; and their youngest daughter, Aldrew, a fine Christian wife and mother, with the same love of Christian education, since she is student counselor for William Woods Junior Woman's Christian College, Fulton, Missouri. Faith has great fruitage!

We first met the Harmons in 1907 at the Minnesota convention. They were resourceful people. Both of them appeared on the convention programs. If they must needs bring the baby and the family along, the one not busy at the moment tended the baby. Also, we have heard that A. D. was forgetful, but that nothing he needed on the pulpit was ever missing; busy wife, mother and preacher when necessary, Alice Gadd Harmon, saw to that.

Dr. A. D. Harmon, as he has been known through years of college leadership, concluded a ministry of fifty-seven years in 1945, his last fruitful pastorate being in the town of Cable, Wisconsin, where his long ministry was to the Congregational-Community Church. Cable is still the Harmons' home town.

Always helpful to the whole Minnesota work, when Dr. Harmon was president of Cotner College, the Harmons helped to develop the Young People's Conference at Tipi Wakan, serving on the faculty from 1920 to 1926.

It was on January 24, 1904, with a temperature at thirty degrees below zero, that the building was dedicated. The church membership was then about 300. Over 400 folk were present at the event. The Portland and Grand Avenue churches of Minneapolis participated. Cash and pledges given that day amounted to $8,689. The entire cost of the building was about $25,000. The old church, moved from Carroll Street, was retained as part of the structure.

Twin City Churches

One must mention the beauty of the First Church. The interior decoration was supervised by Mr. Turner of Mannheimer Brothers. Miss Catherine Ellis, a local artist, painted the beautiful scene at the back of the baptistry, which represents the river Jordan, showing a perspective view of its course for about two miles.

The memorial windows are the work of an outstanding St. Paul artist of those days—R. T. Giles. They are large and very beautiful, one being "The Resurrection," showing Mary and our Lord in the garden of the tomb; the other is Plockhurst's representation of "Behold I stand at the door and knock."

At the time the church was dedicated the pipe organ was not installed. This was dedicated on March 29, 1904, a recital being given by Professor Shuey of the Kimball Organ Company.

Here, then, midway in the history of this church, was the great, decisive victory which must have influenced its whole career.

The year of the dedication the elders of the church were E. T. Gadd (father of Mrs. A. D. Harmon) R. J. McCardy and O. H. Hall; deacons were J. W. Owens, R. Templeman, L. D. Burnett, N. M. Sears, W. U. Smith, E. M. Pierce and E. M. Crandell. The clerk was Everett M. Pierce. Of the names of many faithful we must be silent. It is notable, however, that so many families have remained in the church through the years that the third generation of some of them are to be found in the church today. We would make no mistake in saying that among young people the fourth generation is evident.

Ministers serving after A. D. Harmon were Charles W. Barnes, S. T. Willis, who gave great leadership for six years both in his own church and in the state society; J. D. Howe, E. A. Jordan, R. E. Deadman, Guy V. Ferguson, Virgil R. Walker and Max C. Deweese also served as president of the Minnesota Christian Missionary Society for a short time.

All these ministers helped the church to become great in its local and missionary service as well as in ecumenical matters in its city. The House of the Lord has been cherished and kept as a beautiful place of worship.

Expansion was attempted during the ministry of Mr. Jordan. The church bought lots in the midway district of the Twin

Dr. Andrew Davidson Harmon,
Minnesota Christian Missionary
Society leader.

Alice Gadd Harmon (Mrs. A. D.),
Minnesota Christian Missionary
Society and Christian Woman's
Board of Missions leader.

Charles B. Osgood, Minnesota
Christian Missionary Society leader.

Frank H. Mellen, Minnesota Christian Missionary Society leader.

TWIN CITY CHURCHES

Cities, started a building and made an heroic attempt to have a Midway Christian Church. This was dropped with regret for lack of local support.

The present ministry promises to equal or exceed that of Dr. Harmon. Clarence W. Hautzenrader began his ministry February 18, 1938, together with his wife, Mildred, and little daughter, Janet. In 1941 David Dee, their son, came to them.

On June 5, 1941, the congregation voted to borrow $10,000 and to remodel both buildings, digging a basement under the building first placed on the lot. The present commodious plant, with its beautiful offices, education rooms and parlors cost more than the first amount estimated. Almost in the nature of a Christmas gift to the church of the future, the dedication of these new improvements came on December 14, 1941.

In 1950, still other improvements were added, these costing $10,000. But the church did not stop here. On January 21, 1945, the Hautzenraders moved into their new parsonage, which today is worth $18,000.

State Leadership has been always present in this church. A. D. Harmon led the state board for many years. J. S. Leavitt, layman, has been president of the same board, and Clarence W. Hautzenrader now holds that office. Mr. Hautzenrader has also been president of the St. Paul Interdenominational Council. Mrs. J. S. Leavitt was for more than two years secretary of the Minnesota Women's Missionary Society. Mrs. Hautzenrader has held that office since 1949. In education work in Minnesota and throughout the Brotherhood the Hautzenraders hold a high place.

So, on the hill, within sight of the Roman Catholic Cathedral, stands the church which is a stalwart part of the Protestant forces of St. Paul.

CENTRAL CHURCH, ST. PAUL
(Ramsey County)

Members of the First Church founded the Central Church, St. Paul in 1896. Some of them lived in the section of the city in which the church was located, Leach and McBoal Streets, which was in the neighborhood occupied by several Roman Catholic institutions. The leaders were W. E. Rogers and S. C. Arbuckle, Sr.

Twin City Churches

A neat and adequate corner building which we remember was occupied early in the 20th century by a goodly number of people. Before the dedication of the First Church, in 1904, the state secretary referred in commendatory terms to "the two churches of Minneapolis and the two in St. Paul." He also praised the ministry which all these churches were enjoying.

About 1903 J. H. Bicknell, who had been ministering to the Church of Christ in Liverpool, England, returned to the United States and became minister of the Central Church and State Evangelist for Minnesota. He was a tireless worker. A. D. Harmon said that no man could ring more doorbells in an afternoon than Brother Bicknell. The most thriving season of this church was during his ministry.

Among the members when we first visited this church in 1909 were the two named as leaders, Mrs. W. E. Rogers, Mrs. Elizabeth Hall, and her daughters, Isabel and Maude; Gus and H. F. Heidbrink, Mr. and Mrs. Woodward, Mrs. Kitty Streator, Alice Kirk, Myrtle Johnson, A. L. Winship and Marian Winship. Mrs. W. E. Rogers and Miss Marian Winship were among the missionary leaders of the Twin Cities.

John H. Bicknell left the pastorate to go to Cotner College as registrar in 1911. Following him, John McKee was minister.

Central Church had a goodly number of young people who served in the Christian Endeavor Society and in the choir. They were very resourceful in giving beautiful programs. Two of them went to Cotner College—Alice Kirk and Myrtle Johnson. Isabel Hall became Mrs. H. F. Heidbrink and Maude Mrs. Gus Heidbrink.

After the death of W. E. Rogers, who was the acknowledged leader in the church when your historian knew it, the congregation decided to disband and the building was sold. So far as we remember this happened about the close of the first World War. The most active people went into the First Church—Mrs. Elizabeth Hall, the H. F. and Gus Heidbrink families, Mrs. W. E. Rogers, Marian Winship, Mrs. Streator and the Woodwards all found their places at once in the sister church. There may have been others also. A number of Central young people had moved away by this time.

A designated fund from Central Church was distributed by First Church for some time. Part of it went, at intervals, to

TWIN CITY CHURCHES

the Twin City Union (an organization of the Twin City woman's missionary societies) and part to the Minnesota Christian Missionary Society.

PORTLAND AVENUE CHURCH, MINNEAPOLIS
(Hennepin County)

As we approach the history of this church we think of GREAT-HEARTED people. It is from the history written by Dr. David Owen Thomas in 1922 that we find our facts to that date, though we first entered the doors of this church in the State Convention, 1907.

In this masterly statement of the genius of the Disciples of Christ, as it motivated the founders of this church, Dr. Thomas says, "The church in its ideals and achievements is a fair representative of the religious movement to which it belongs, called the Reformation of the Nineteenth Century, as urged by the Disciples of Christ. . . . They had brought with them the exalted vision of unity, freedom, and fellowship of a church organized on the Scriptures alone, without any sectarian barriers, accepting no name but that of Christ, imposing no terms of church membership except confessed faith and complete obedience to Jesus Christ, administering the two sacraments of the New Testament in the way approved by our Lord, and pleading for Christian Union on the original basis, by restoring the church to the primitive model of the apostolic days in doctrine, fellowship, and life."

Dr. Thomas and Mrs. Thomas, whose maiden name was Ann Butler, united with the church in 1885, coming from Indianapolis, Indiana. Dr. Thomas has written books on the Lord's Supper, showing himself to be a theologian as well as a spiritually-minded Christian.

On February 14, 1877, in the home of Mr. and Mrs. A. T. Ankeny, the following persons met to organize themselves into a congregation. The Ankenys, Mrs. Wyman, Mr. and Mrs. R. T. Beebe, Mr. and Mrs. S. B. Mattison and Mrs. Sarah D. Atkinson. At that time Professor Atkinson, who previously occupied the chair of mathematics Hiram College, was an invalid and unable to attend. Also, Mrs. B. F. Hazeltine, another charter member, was away because of illness. At the invitation of this group John La Grange, a Baptist minister who understood our church well, helped in the organization of the little company.

As the church met in homes they were soon joined by others, J. W. Birdwell, a great Bible teacher who had heard Alexander Campbell preach, was one of these.

All these people and others who joined them would have found a place in any Protestant evangelical church in Minneapolis had they desired to do so, but their belief that they had a religious contribution to make to the Protestant faith in Minnesota caused them to form their own church.

February 25, 1887, found them meeting at the Swedenborgian church on 9th Street and 5th Avenue South. On March 28th of the same year the Ladies' Aid Society was first organized and the women called Elder N. A. McConnell of Cedar Rapids, Iowa, to preach for them. Quoting again from Dr. Thomas' record—"Twenty-three signed a covenant to meet every Lord's Day, to keep the ordinances, and to call themselves the Church of Christ."

After that pastors and evangelists were E. T. C. Bennett, W. H. Rogers, a student at the Minnesota University, and L. J. Bailey, who, with Dr. and Mrs. L. W. Denton conducting music, succeeded in bringing over twenty people into the church.

At the time of their first regular minister—John Hay, Charles Evans Holt, a new convert, dealer in real estate, found the lot on Portland and Grant Streets, 125 feet, priced at $2,100. This seemed a lot of money, but the people ventured. Mr. Holt purchased a wooden tabernacle from the Hennepin Avenue Methodist Church, complete with furnishings, carpet and pulpit. This was moved to the lot as the first church home. After Mr. Hay left, J. H. Garrison, editor of *The Christian-Evangelist*, spent some weeks with the church.

In 1883 Enos Campbell, a cousin of Alexander Campbell and a graduate of Bethany College, became minister. The church grew rapidly. About this time Mr. A. E. Major and his family united with the church. His daughters, Leta Major Pickett and Laura Lynne Major became missionaries, the former to the Philippines and the latter to China. The Campbells were

TWIN CITY CHURCHES

great missionary people. In their time the Christian Woman's Board of Missions auxiliary was organized and Mrs. Campbell led a large Missions Band for Juniors.

It was in the ministry of W. J. Lhamon, a graduate of Butler College, that the first part of the building now being used was dedicated. The church and the large Christian Endeavor Society had to meet elsewhere during that summer. The lecture room and other rooms were roofed over and dedicated in the second year of Mr. Lhamon's ministry, which lasted from 1887 to 1894, and which was a time of great growth for the church. Mr. and Mrs. C. H. Slack became members during this time. Mr. Slack, an attorney, helped the State Board in later years in legal matters. He was noted for his talks to ministers on "The Preacher and The Law," believing that the minister should know God's Law and the laws of his country, as they related to church property and congregational procedure.

The prayer meetings of this season were times of great discussion. Dr. Thomas in his history says that sometimes they almost grew into debates, since each watched the other to see if he was true to the teachings of the Disciples of Christ. Perhaps this irked the women. Dr. Thomas speaks of Mr. Smith Covey, who at one time explained some doctrinal point only to have his wife say, "You are right, Smith, but sit down."

We pause here to mention some interesting persons named as having filled the pulpit during early days. One of them is Cyrus Northrup, President of the University of Minnesota. Those named as having held short evangelistic meetings are I. N. McCash and W. F. Richardson. Dr. H. L. Willett also was a visiting minister.

During the ministry of Carey E. Morgan 1894-1899 the superstructure was built, making a beautiful church. We think that some parts were added to the basement at this time. Two memorial windows were placed in the sanctuary, one to the memory of Enos and Mary Campbell and another to Mrs. C. E. Wyman. The property was worth about $50,000. It was dedicated, with F. M. Rains officiating, February 10, 1895, and that day $12,975 was given.

A daring thing happened in the ministry of C. J. Tanner, 1900-1903. In 1901 there came to Minneapolis the National

TWIN CITY CHURCHES

Convention of the Disciples of Christ. It was not easy to bring such a gathering as far out as Minnesota, and it was the vision of the young people of the church who led in the movement to bring it. In the published material used to advertise the convention locally, a design bearing these words was used, "MINNEAPOLIS TWENTIETH CENTURY CHRISTIAN CHURCH MISSIONARY CONVENTION, OCTOBER 10-17." Registrations reached over 2700 and the church felt proud and well repaid.

Mr. Tanner had great financial ability and it was in 1902 that the debt on the building was paid. A "revival" led by Charles Reign Scoville and De Loss Smith added one hundred twenty-six people to the church.

Even greater than that was the expansion in Minneapolis, causing Portland Avenue to become "THE MOTHER CHURCH." Mr. E. S. Wood, from 1901, had been conducting a Sunday school in southeast Minneapolis, which afterward became the University Place Church. On October 5, 1902, the Grand Avenue Christian Church was dedicated, a comfortable building on 31st Street South and Grand Avenue. Gladly the mother church gave fifty-five members, to become the charter members of the new church. So went the onward march of the Disciples of Christ in Minneapolis.

During the ministry of R. W. Abberly, 1903-1906, an English-man, graduate of Cotner College, the pipe organ now being used was purchased. The James Small revival was held, bring-ing still more people into the church. The Ladies' Aid was adding much to the church finances, having an enrollment of eighty-eight.

Perry J. Rice became minister in 1906 and remained until 1909. He, too, led in another outreach. H. D. Kitson, a lay-man, and Mr. and Mrs. C. H. Durose, who already lived in the new Minnehaha section of the city, started a Sunday school. At length Mr. Rice organized the Minnehaha Christian Church. Once more, members of the Portland Avenue Church were gladly given to extend Disciple borders in the growing city.

From 1912 to 1918 S. Grundy Fisher gave a fruitful minis-try. He was active in the State work and a leader in the City Missions Board of Minneapolis which was organized about 1916. Mr. Fisher and his church gave excellent leadership

TWIN CITY CHURCHES

and financial support in organizing the Lake Harriet Church and the Audubon Park Church. Thus Portland Avenue had given most of the leadership in planting five churches in the first two decades of the 20th century.

For a short time Ada L. Forster served as associate minister with Mr. Fisher and when he left in December, 1917, to serve in Young Men's Christian Association work, in the first World War, she led the church for six months.

The church first became a living link, supporting Miss Mary Campbell as missionary to India in 1920, when S. Gershon Bennett was minister. About 1920, also, Mrs. Irene Davis became minister's assistant, which position she still occupies, having given thirty years of good service.

Robert H. Newton served as minister from 1922 to 1926. There was continued talk of moving to a new location, or extending the building for educational purposes. However, it was in the time of George O. Marsh, 1926-1937, that the fine addition the church now has was made, as well as other alterations for both beauty and utility.

The present ministry, that of Forrest L. Richeson, has seen the church come to such great growth that a much larger building is necessary and possible. Dr. Richeson's ministry is the longest yet given to this church. In his years the church has renewed its youth, literally. Always the largest giver to State Missions, the harvest is NOW, in that its membership contains wonderful families who have come from almost every village and town church in Minnesota.

The old time and the new were linked, early in the present ministry, in the payment of a bequest made by Mrs. David Owen Thomas, of $10,000. This paid off the remaining debt of renovation of the church and set up a fund for the proposed new building.

Each year pledges are asked for the building fund. These are just made to be paid in 1952, in the amount of over $44,000.

There is no better central location than the ten lots, about one acre and a half, purchased by the church for $40,000, on Twenty-second Street and First Avenue South. The beautiful Minneapolis Art Institute stands within sight of it. Here will be erected a building which will cost approximately $500,000.

TWIN CITY CHURCHES

Plans are being drawn and surely, not long after the seventy-fifth anniversary of the church (1952), this building will be a fact.

In leaving this story, we find a great church of 875 resident members. The staff has three full-time workers, with others employed on occasions, and with lay leadership which has, over and over again, fulfilled the desire of the pioneers that our people "do exploits" in what they considered to be the "Reformation Movement" of the 19th century.

So may Dorothy and Forrest Richeson, and this church, go on in abundant missionary giving, as leaders in our national church life, in ecumenical church affairs, and in the civic life of Minneapolis.

GRAND AVENUE CHURCH, MINNEAPOLIS, 1902-1923

(Hennepin County)

On October 5, 1902, the Grand Avenue Christian Church, 31st Street and Grand Avenue, Minneapolis, was dedicated. This was done by the sacrificial planning of the Portland Avenue Church, during the ministry of C. J. Tanner. Fifty-five members of the "mother" church were spared to lead that church, most of them living in the neighborhood. Among the charter members were the F. H. Mellen and A. E. Major families.

The church at one time had a membership of almost 300, it did a great Sunday school work and also was truly a missionary church. Among its ministers were C. B. Osgood, H. C. Connelly, Ray E. Hunt and A. D. Brokaw. When, in 1923, the building was eventually sold, its membership enriched other churches, giving leadership at Portland Avenue, Lake Harriet and Minnehaha. This church gave Burton L. Hoffman to the ministry. It continues its blessing to this day, especially in efficient leadership in Lake Harriet Church.

UNIVERSITY PLACE CHURCH, MINNEAPOLIS

(Hennepin County)

Mr. and Mrs. E. S. Wood and family of the Portland Avenue Church started a Sunday School on Central Avenue in the southeast part of Minneapolis, probably about 1900.

Twin City Churches

It is evident that a church adjacent to the University was in the minds of our people, part of the growth always intended in Minneapolis. The work of Mr. and Mrs. E. S. Wood was carried over to the University Place Church.

The State Board and American Christian Missionary Society were interested helpers in providing ministers in the early days. We remember John McKee and Grover C. Schurman as ministers, between 1911-1913, when the meeting place was 4th Street and 17th Avenue Southeast. We have a list of membership, about 1913, which includes 87 names. Among the families were students of the University of Minnesota.

After the building of the first unit of the Minneapolis Bible College the church sold its property in behalf of that building. It became the home of students and faculty, who through the years have often given service in preaching and in the beautiful music that the church has used in its worship. Frequently the minister has also been a member of the faculty of the Bible College, as was the case with W. J. Carry, John Christofferson and W. T. Fisher. In later years, however, the minister has not usually been a member of the faculty. The present minister, Arthur Poll, is a graduate of the Bible College. The sanctuary in which the congregation worships is stately, one of which any church can be proud.

For some time after the church moved to the college the Woman's Missionary Society of the Christian Woman's Board of Missions continued and some of the members were on the Minnesota Board of that organization. The church also remained cooperative with our State and National Missionary Boards until about 1918. Since then "independent" missions only have been supported. For some time the church led in keeping two young men, former students, in Poland.

They now support the missions to which the students of the Bible College give service.

Minnehaha Church, Minneapolis

The initial work in this church was the second venture made by the Portland Avenue Church in a new section of Minneapolis. Members who had moved to this southeast section joined in making beautiful the territory near to Minnehaha Falls and the famous park around these Falls.

TWIN CITY CHURCHES

Perry J. Rice, minister of the Portland Avenue Church, with
H. D. Kitson and Verne Crowl, young laymen, and Miss Mary
Drake a schoolteacher, gave their services in organizing a
Sunday school. The meeting place was in a hall on East
Forty-fifth Street. No other church served this territory, which
was largely a Scandinavian section. This hall was used for
dances on Saturday nights and had to be made ready for
Sunday afternoon school.

September 19, 1909, this Sunday school was organized. At
that time the C. H. Durose and W. Z. Adams families, hitherto
members of Portland Avenue, declared their intention of making
Minnehaha their church home.

Mrs. Adams and Mrs. Durose organized a Ladies' Aid Society, also late in 1909. This society enlisted many women in
the neighborhood and began at once to obtain funds for a
church home.

Every Sunday afternoon, after Sunday school, the Lord's
Table was spread. When no minister was available, C. H.
Durose made people acquainted with the message of the Dis-
ciples of Christ in his talks at the Table. Gradually people
were enlisted, many of them having former Lutheran affiliation.
Two years later, the first minister, A. W. Van Dervort said,
"The twelfth ward is half Socialist, and the immediate neigh-
borhood is at least 75% Scandinavian Lutheran. The majority,
members of other communions, never heard of the Christian
Church. Conditions make it necessary for us to grow a church.
Already 50% of our members came as the direct result of the
Sunday school."

Perry J. Rice was appreciated for his fine advice to the
coming church. The minister following him was appointed by
the Portland Avenue Church as head of a building committee
for Minnehaha, with two businessmen, M. R. Waters and
Charles Oliver, together with H. D. Kitson, then State Secretary, and C. H. Durose as committee. In 1910 the double lot
on 42nd Street and 32nd Avenue South was purchased. Doctor
George D. Haggard was appointed as an advisory member of
their church board, which position he held for about seven
years. He was a welcome advisor, always.

Mr. Van Dervort was called as minister in October, 1911. In
January, 1912, after a meeting held by John G. Slayter, the
church was organized, with 56 charter members, fourteen from

TWIN CITY CHURCHES

Portland Avenue, two from Grand Avenue, seven from other churches and thirty-three by baptism. By November of that year, after a meeting held by H. G. Connelly, of Grand Avenue Church, the membership grew to seventy.

When the church was erected in 1912, it was, like many other buildings in the neighborhood, covered on the outside with tar paper. Its first seats were boards stretched across nail kegs. Through the unfinished streets of the neighborhood the people waded in mud, often bringing their own lanterns, which were always useful to help light the church. Sometimes they each donated fuel in the cold winter weather.

Mr. Van Dervort was the living link of the Portland Avenue Church, through the American Christian Missionary Society. He was a great social worker, as well as minister, working much among the boys' gangs of the neighborhood and, at times, in Juvenile Court with them. Mr. Van Dervort married soon after coming to Minneapolis, to Anna Robinette, a neice of Mrs. Anna R. Atwater, and found his wife a great helper. They remained with Minnehaha for over six years.

The church carried a great program. In 1911-1912 there were fifty regular givers. By that year, too, there were 222 enrolled in the Sunday school, exclusive of 42 on the Cradle Roll, and the average attendance was 178. The Board of Deaconesses not only did their usual church work, but became leaders in charitable work outside. The choir, always a great organization in this church, was organized. Evening services, large Christian Endeavor Society, Wednesday prayer meetings were all well attended and constantly new people were added.

Organized labor in the neighborhood threatened the peace of the church when, both in its initial building, and as it was finished, much of the work was done by members. A. W. Van Dervort's tact saved the day.

By the early twenties the Sunday school attendance grew to between three and four hundred. Frank S. Bartlett, Jr., was then minister. Under his leadership a second loan was obtained from the Church Board of Extension and the "annex," an educational unit, was built, and the whole building improved. Beautiful pews replaced the chairs of the sanctuary. All in all, there was two-thirds more space made for the education program. By this time several Lutheran churches had come

TWIN CITY CHURCHES

into the neighborhood, yet Minnehaha's Sunday school drew the young life of the section. Added were a Boy Scout Troop and other youth organizations.

The "depression" of the early thirties retarded payment of the loan and the building became run down. From 1935 to 1945 the whole building was renovated, and plans made for regular payment of the debt. Much of the beautiful furniture of the sanctuary came from memorial gifts, including the electric organ. Ada L. Forster was minister during this period. She was followed by Gilford Olmsted and it was in early 1946, during his ministry, that the long-standing mortgage was burned. At the close of his ministry the parsonage, beautiful in its location, was purchased.

So Minnehaha Church marches on. In a 1942 count, there were twenty-nine people in official positions in the church, who had been the Sunday School children of early days. The new goal is to rebuild part of the church. Gordon W. Hagberg carries on its tradition of having a well-prepared ministry. A. W. Van Dervort's plan to "grow our own church" became true.

Minnehaha's ministers have always been of fine type. Besides those mentioned above there were: L. A. Brumbaugh; the seven-year ministry of LaVerne Morris; J. L. McBean and W. W. Wilson, all of whom added greatly to the growth of the church.

LAKE HARRIET CHURCH, MINNEAPOLIS

Into a far more settled neighborhood, after a meeting with the comity committee of the interdenominational forces of Minneapolis, Portland Avenue once more launched out into the beautiful Lake Harriet district, in southwest Minneapolis. A number of church families had moved to this section.

About the same time a group of people were pleading for a church in northeast Minneapolis. In this location is today's Audubon Park Church.

It was thought best to organize the City Missions Board of Minneapolis, and to have this body lead in the work, all the churches belonging to it. Most of the funds, at first, came from Portland Avenue. "City Missions" remained for about 20 years, providing a great bond of fellowship for Minneapolis

TWIN CITY CHURCHES

churches. M. M. Moss was the first secretary, following him was David Shield. C. B. Osgood served as its last missionary, from 1930 to 1934.

The Lake Harriet Church was organized in 1916, with twelve families on its charter roll. C. C. Crouch, E. M. Hanson and D. D. Lester became elders. All the families were folk of great talent, and perfect records were kept by Mrs. Gail Westberg, for many years secretary.

Their first meeting place was in a theater. However, by June, 1917, there was dedicated a bungalow type church, on 46th Street West and Washburn Avenue South. M. M. Moss, with his own hands, helped on this building and he ministered to the church. The efficient elders were also part-time ministers.

In these days much was made of the Sunday school. C. C. Crouch built up a class for men, great in numbers and interest. Not all of them stayed to morning worship, but growth came through this class. Mr. Crouch also became president of the Minnesota Christian Missionary Society. From the first of its history Lake Harriet has supplied personnel for City, State and interdenominational work.

In 1923, when the Grand Avenue Church discontinued its work in that location, many families joined with Lake Harriet, families who had given leadership as officers, musicians, in women's and men's work, and as Sunday school teachers. These added great strength to the church. It was in that year that the present location, at 50th Street and Beard Avenue South, was secured and the first section of the present building erected. Later the chapel was moved from the first location and placed upon the basement building. Always there was the intention to finish the church that it might be a thing of beauty in this genteel part of Minneapolis. As families moved to this section our church was further enriched by our own people, and it also drew many from its neighborhood. Many names might be mentioned, but we cannot even begin, so great are they all in service. Their recent history proclaims their fine stewardship. Ministers who have led them in later years have been Rob Roy Hardin, Randall Lookabill, Paul Rains, Loren Jenks, O. Eugene Moore, Kenneth B. Ball, and the present minister is J. Bryant Young. During the ministry of Mr. Moore a parsonage was purchased.

TWIN CITY CHURCHES

On November 12, 1950, there was dedicated the dream church of many years. The little bungalow church was moved away, the basement floor building enlarged and improved, and the stately sanctuary, with added rooms on the same floor, dedicated. Dr. Gaines N. Cook was the preaching guest. State representatives, other Christian churches, and neighborhood churches were participating guests.

There are nineteen churches in the evangelical fellowship in this district, one of them the Mt. Olivet Lutheran, led by Dr. Rueben K. Youngdahl, who was a guest at the dedication. These churches work closely together. So in a comparatively few years the Lake Harriet Church has its property worth $125,000 and, greater still, its place in the ecumenical work of Minneapolis, as well as in all the aims and projects of the Disciples of Christ.

AUDUBON PARK CHURCH, MINNEAPOLIS

This church is, in most ways, the contemporary of Lake Harriet. They shared the same minister at the time of their organization, M. M. Moss, Minneapolis City Missionary. Prior to the time they acquired their own property, families who lived in northeast and southeast Minneapolis met in homes and their first incorporation was known as The Van Cleve Church of Christ, in southeast Minneapolis.

After canvassing the city for a good location, it was decided that, if we were to follow our usual procedure in planting churches in different districts of Minneapolis, we must go northeast. The lot on 28th Street and Lincoln Street Northeast was therefore purchased. The name of the church was then changed to Audubon Park. The church met in the home of Mr. and Mrs. E. S. Owen, in the northeast section, while the building was being completed.

With the help of the City Missions' organization, which was a project of the American Christian Missionary Society, as well as that of the churches in Minneapolis, and also of the Church Extension Board, a portable building was purchased, set up, and dedicated November 11, 1916. Mr. and Mrs. Richard Todd, the only couple married in this building, are still serving the church.

TWIN CITY CHURCHES

Until 1925 this building served and at that time the basement part of the permanent building was started, this being dedicated early in 1926. It might be said here that the portable was purchased by the State Board and sent on flat cars to Hollandale, where for a time we had a church.

When the Portland Avenue Church was remodeled, about 1931, the Communion Table and chairs were given to Audubon Park Church, which later passed them on to the Fargo, North Dakota, church.

In 1943, when Wilbur Watkins was minister, the property next door to the church was purchased to be used as a parsonage. This gave the church a great lift and stabilized its whole program. Bonds, bricks and war bonds were sold to pay for this home and in 1945 the mortgage was burned.

Free of debt, the church launched out to build the superstructure of their church. One of their own members, Chester Glisen, was the contractor. The building, including Hammond electric organ, pulpit furniture and pews, was not to exceed $25,000.

John G. Olmsted, who succeeded Wilbur Watkins, spent the last years of his ministry, before retirement, with this church. To the present pastor, Wallace W. Pomplun, goes the honor of leading in the final property victory. The sanctuary has "blond" finish throughout, giving a beautiful effect. Other rooms on this upper floor are pastor's study and classrooms, making splendid education facilities.

No church in the Twin Cities has come to victory through as hard and uphill a road as Audubon. Often few in numbers, at times not having regular and full-time ministry, with salaried folk in the church and no well-to-do members, these brave people have entered their 34th year of service. They have been missionary all the way, taking their due part in all brotherhood projects. Their future is assured.

FORTY-EIGHTH STREET CHURCH, MINNEAPOLIS

In the early twenties, E. M. Hanson and others of the Lake Harriet Church saw an opportunity to enter another field in South Minneapolis, mid-way between Lake Harriet and Minnehaha. This became another project of City Missions.

TWIN CITY CHURCHES

The first Sunday school met near the location of the church —Forty-eighth Street and Portland Avenue, in the home of Mrs. Dysie Brader, and thus there was gathered together sufficient people to warrant buying a schoolhouse, which stood on several fine corner lots at the above location, with the help of the Board of Church Extension.

Frequently the ministry of the Forty-eighth Street Church had to be part time or given by one who had other means of livelihood. It was during such a ministry, given by James C. Brown, that the beautiful sanctuary, formerly one of the schoolrooms, was furnished, making this imposing building a good church home. Though a layman at that time, Mr. Brown was a graduate of Eureka College, having ministerial training.

Though the section was not overchurched, the work has not grown as have other Minneapolis churches. The State Board now holds the property, at the request of former members. Ministering at this time is Ray Kegley, a layman with ministerial training and former student of Minneapolis Bible College.

Since the property is adequate, there may still be a greater future for this church.

DULUTH

(St. Louis County)

We do not find as much available on this church as we would wish. However, it was organized in 1886. The first minister is referred to as Reverend Sharp and the frame building occupied at that time was on 12th Avenue West and Superior Street. Two years later they moved to the building which was the home of the church through many years, on 5th Avenue West and 4th Street. So far as we can get the names of the charter members they are: Mrs. Victor Dash and family, Mr. and Mrs. O. L. Young, Henry Grieser, The Austin family (whom we remember as most earnest workers but whose first names we do not have), Mr. and Mrs. E. R. Cobb, the Henderson family, a family named Spearin, Mrs. Charles Older, Thomas Tidball and family, John Tidball and family, Neal Hendricks and family, whose son is Mr. Kenneth C. Hendricks, missionary to Japan; Mrs. I. Ridge, W. F. Davies and family, Mr. and Mrs. Josiah Eby, three sisters whose name was Wagoner, one of them was

DULUTH

Miss Lura whom we remember as an ardent missionary worker; Clara Smart, Grace Holden, Mrs. Alvina Reid (many years at Portland Avenue Church, and housekeeper at Tipi Wakan), Mr. and Mrs. Archie Gish, the Swan family, whose son, Frank, was for some years a deacon, Dr. Maxwell and family, Mrs. J. Wanless, Margaret and George Essen. Later, the Charles Evans Holt and E. A. Risdon families were of great service to the church.

Among early ministers we find Robert Grieve and J. K. Shellenberger, who served so long and well in the state. Some others were Ben Mitchell, M. B. Ainsworth, Baxter Waters, Bruce Black and S. W. Nay.

Roy E. Hunt became minister in 1910. During his ministry the church decided to locate in a new neighborhood. The basement was finished and roofed on 12th Avenue East and 4th Street. It was commodious and gave promise of being the first part of a beautiful building. The church seemed much encouraged. This move gave a better district in which to work. It was the neighborhood in which most of the members lived.

In the early twenties, during the ministry of Dr. S. T. Willis, plans were drawn and accepted by a building committee to build the superstructure; however, Dr. Willis' health was not good and he was obliged to leave before the work started. We think of him as a great servant of the church. He and Mr. Hunt were among the most useful persons in the state work.

The Duluth church was always interested in our missionary work and their women leaders gave state-wide service. Among them were Mrs. R. G. Mace and Mrs. Lee Rickey. There were also laymen who served on our State Board.

Homer J. Armstrong, who was helping the State Board, supported by the Home Department of the United Christian Missionary Society, went to confer with the pastorless church in Duluth in 1928. The congregation had become discouraged, chiefly because of the delay in their building plans. Being urged by the congregation, he accepted the pastorate.

In 1929, the Baptist church of Duluth being then pastorless, it seemed well to Mr. Armstrong to canvass the possibility of the two churches joining together for service. There was some thought at the time this was done that the Christian church

DULUTH

location might become the place of meeting for the united church, and that plans made in Dr. Willis' time be used to complete the building.

The plan for unity was made, and Mr. Armtsrong became minister of the "United Church, Baptist and Disciple," in which position he remained until 1936. During these years Mr. Armstrong gave leadership among young people in the Tipi Wakan Conference. He was much beloved by the young people, influencing the lives of many. Tipi Wakan became the conference attended by Duluth youth, both Baptist and Disciples.

The Baptist church building being large and adequate, it was finally decided to use that as the church home. Our building on 12th Avenue East and 4th Street was sold, the proceeds being used for Disciple work.

Until this time, the plan of designating missionary offerings has been used. Thus the offerings of those with Christian church affiliation may always go to their own missionary boards.

Since Mr. Armstrong's time two ministers have served the church, J. F. Pennington and the present minister, Frank See. Both of them have a Baptist background. However, they have given themselves to service in the Minnesota Christian Missionary Society and have understood, and advanced, the work of all our missions.

The United Church has become a powerful organization in Duluth, and one feels that the witness of the Disciples of Christ has been maintained.

AUSTIN

(Mower County)

On July 4, 1897, Vernon J. Rose and Ernest Kerr, evangelists, led in the organization of the Austin Church. This was a good beginning in a growing town. In a beautiful farming section, home of the Hormel Meat Packing Company and other industries, our church was well placed.

Charter members were: Warren S. Kennedy, Kate Kennedy, Hannah E. Snyder, Henry H. Codding, Charles S. Codding, Mrs. H. M. Hickcock, D. S. Mosher, Maria Watkins and Lulu R. Ward.

AUSTIN

The first building was purchased in 1899 and sold in 1902. The second building, a neat structure, was obtained in 1906, both of these being acquired from other church communions.

The State evangelist, A. B. Moore, was acting pastor for a short time. Then, from November 26, 1899, to January 1, 1900, evangelists J. S. Miller and R. A. Givens held a protracted meeting and many were added to the church. M. C. Johnson served as minister. He remained for about a year. Other ministers serving to the early twenties were John Treleau, Charles Forster, H. M. Johnson, B. H. Wharton, C. A. Park, A. L. Ogden and Dow Crewdson.

State Secretary J. H. Bicknell and Evangelist C. R. Neal were of much help to the church from 1906 to 1911, as was C. B. Osgood in a later day. In this period the O. C. Heilman family, afterward active in Fargo, North Dakota, were among the leaders, also the J. C. Hall family. Mrs. Heilman and Mrs. Hall were leaders in the Woman's Missionary Society, which was one of the most active in southern Minnesota. Mrs. Ethel Hall Horn was organist for many years. Mr. and Mrs. O. S. Avery served this church for many years.

In 1917 the church had grown in numbers and program and a new building was necessary. The present building, far more adequate and beautiful than those preceding it, was dedicated January 20, 1918. Secretary C. B. Osgood and his son Howard were of much help at this time and they took part in the event. Arthur Scott was the minister at the time of the building program. George L. Snively officiated at the dedication.

In May, 1924, Harry Poll, student of the Minnesota Bible College, began the longest pastorate in the history of the church, remaining until July, 1940. Mr. Poll's graduation came in 1927 at which time the family became resident. His work with the church in stewardship was admirable and set the pace that has been followed ever since.

Just before the close of Mr. Poll's ministry the house next door to the church was purchased and connected to the church by an underground passage.

Austin gave help also, during Mr. Poll's ministry, to the Hollandale church, when the State Board shipped a portable building, which had been used by Audubon Park Church in Minneapolis, to Hollandale. This was redeemed swamp land,

AUSTIN

sold in a big boom for growing potatoes, onions and celery. Later, however, the project failed, people gave up their land and, we think, a few families went to the Austin church.

Ministers following Mr. Poll were C. Max Buck, C. C. McCaw, who did a splendid work in the church and who was also very helpful in the State Society, Charles Davis and the present minister, Herman Kooy, a graduate of the Minnesota Bible College.

Recently the church withdrew support from the Minnesota Christian Missionary Society, which made its program completely "independent." Its membership, we understand, is still well over three hundred. The missionary support is wholly to "independent" missions.

STERLING CHURCH, AUSTIN

(Mower County)

Changes in policy of the Austin Church caused about fifty persons, who wished to remain in harmony with the Minnesota Christian Missionary Society and our National Missionary Boards, to enter into consideration of what is now known as the Sterling Christian Church, Austin, Minnesota.

They first organized themselves into the Austin Christian Study Group. On February 11, 1949, this group discussed with Vernon Stagner, the State Secretary, the advisability of investigating the southwest section of Austin with the intention to found a new church. This is a growing section, composed largely of new dwellings and the group was ready to determine how many unchurched folk might be residing there.

In their canvass they sought the help of Reverend Joe Chapman, the northern Baptist State leader. On April 8, 1949, Mr. Chapman, with Vernon Stagner and Wallace Pomplun, minister of the Audubon Park Church, Minneapolis, made sufficient investigation of the section to know that a thorough census of the neighborhood was warranted. On May 15, workers of the two communions began the canvass and finished it before the end of the month. Though no local Baptists were found to come into the church at that time, the State Baptist Board expressed willingness to help in the new

STERLING CHURCH, AUSTIN

project. The findings of the canvass are in the hands of the Minnesota Christian Missionary Society and the Baptist State Board.

The Minnesota Christian Missionary Society voted to make Sterling Church a "Crusade" project. By July 1, 1950, Wendell Pew of Minneapolis, a student at Drake University, was called as minister.

On August 6, 1950, the Study Group organized the Sterling Christian Church, with forty-one members. May 1, 1951, there were forty-six members. These members are devoted to the church and have much in Christian faith, combined with great talent, to give to the new work. Their young minister is the grandson of Mr. and Mrs. S. C. Pew, charter members of the Fairmont Church and of the same family as W. W. Pew, a pioneer leader in Minnesota.

In 1950, also, a beautiful corner site was purchased, which includes four lots, at a cost of $5,433, made up of Crusade money, gifts of the membership and of the Portland Avenue Church, Minneapolis.

While funds were being accumulated for the building the church met in the Austin Theatre for Sunday school and Morning Worship. The management made no rental charge. A $30,000 church building was completed in October of 1952.

Meanwhile, there is a well-organized church board, a strong Christian Women's Fellowship, and a youth group which meets Sunday evenings. At intervals, workers' conferences have been held. The weekly offerings are entirely meeting current expense needs and the missionary giving has been very commendable and regular. All in all the progress has been unusual and the future of such a group seems thoroughly assured.

Mrs. W. K. Evans, of the Sterling Church, is the President of the Minnesota Christian Women's Fellowship.

CROOKSTON

(Polk County)

We have been unable to get the exact date of the founding of this church but we remember well the occasion.

About 1917 Crookston was recommended as a town in which we should organize a church. Help was forthcoming at that

CROOKSTON

time from the Christian Woman's Board of Missions for a new work and C. B. Osgood, then State Secretary, went to survey the field. The church was organized, Mr. Osgood remaining on the field for several months and acting as minister.

Meetings were held for some time in homes and halls that were available. There were some fine leaders, among them Drs. Fred and Blanche Sharp, Professor and Mrs. T. M. McCall, Mr. and Mrs. H. M. McFarlin, Mrs. McWaters and her family. We wish we had a full list of the folk of that day.

Professor McCall is still a leader in the State Agricultural College in Crookston, and active in the church, as are the Drs. Sharp, Mrs. McWaters, whose two sons are among the leaders in the Sunday school and Church Board. Mrs. Carroll H. Lemon, of Lincoln, Nebraska, was formerly Miss Myrtle McWaters of this church.

When Mr. Osgood must needs go on to other fields, W. J. Carry, who had been minister at Staples, was called to be the first minister of the new church. The Christian Woman's Board of Missions continued to finance part of the minister's salary.

As soon as it was possible a good lot was purchased and a church building erected. We remember that it was an adequate structure and well arranged.

A Woman's Missionary Society did fine work. Mrs. W. J. Carry was a leader in this society, as were other ladies already named.

A Mr. DeLapp, leader when the church was founded, who was also conducting a business college in Crookston, made rooms available to the church before the building was finished. We regret not having his initials. He was a good servant of the church.

Among the ministers following W. J. Carry were L. H. Benny and Leonard H. Camp. Students of the Minnesota Bible College have served as ministers. The present minister is Randall L. Barnes, who is also a teacher in the local high school. His parents were formerly members of the church in Fairmont, Martin County. Besides C. B. Osgood, Evangelist L. C. McPherson gave a number of months' service to this church in 1919-1920. We regret that the church of today, so close to the State Society in earlier years, now makes no reports to the State office.

FAIRMONT

(Martin County)

The first organization in Fairmont came in 1897, under the leadership of David Husband, an evangelist of the Christian church. At this meeting George Schultz was chairman and Dr. Emeline Tanner, secretary. Others present were George Tanner, R. M. Longstreet, Mr. and Mrs. J. H. Longstreet, P. S. Hicks, and Mrs. E. J. Thompson. Meetings of the group evidently did not continue. We subsequently knew that some of the above persons worked with Methodist and Congregational churches, with the understanding that when they were able to continue with their own church they would do so.

Under the direction of J. M. Dixon, a Christian minister, the present organization was completed on September 14, 1905. Elders elected were George Tanner and C. R. Pew; deacons, R. M. Longstreet and S. C. Pew; deaconess, Mrs. E. J. Thompson and Dr. Emeline Tanner. Trustees were C. R. Pew, George Ott and J. H. Fowler. Dr. Emeline Tanner was elected as clerk.

A place of meeting was the first consideration. A lot was secured at once for $200 and a $10 payment made. Horican church was not at that time meeting in the building and there was some thought of securing and removing it. Fortunately this was not done. Finally a hall over the restaurant, known as Daniel's Hall, became the church home. This was no ideal place. However, the church had it wired for electric lighting, curtained off for church school departments, installed a temporary baptistry, repaired and cleaned so well that, despite noise and heat in summertime, this hall was the beloved church home for more than eight years.

In 1905-1906 J. P. Childs became minister. For some time after this E. A. Hiett, a layman, preached. On July 21, 1907, Ada L. Forster became minister, remaining until September, 1911.

Under the leadership of Dr. Emeline Tanner, a fully graded Sunday school had more than one hundred in attendance by 1907, and many more later. A large Christian Endeavor Society made the number of people meeting in the Sunday school and Christian Endeavor over 200 each week. These meetings were full of enthusiasm. Services were well attended.

FAIRMOUNT

In March, 1908, it was decided to buy building and loan stock. The lot already mentioned was paid for. A church which was for sale in town was considered. These were some of the many attempts to build which were made in early days. The church was all the time being strengthened. Mr. and Mrs. C. S. White came from What Cheer, Iowa, in 1907. They were great leaders. Many young people came through the Sunday school and the church was "grown," taking its place for good in Fairmont. Evangelists helping in this growth, from 1907 to 1911, were Alden Lee Hill, minister of the Truman church, J. H. Bicknell, A. J. Hollingsworth and John Olmsted.

The church had developed good lay leadership. These, with some ad interim ministers, served until W. R. Burton became minister in April, 1913. The Organ-Howe evangelistic company held a meeting, at the close of which plans were made to build. The first lot was sold and another in a better location bought. The cost of the building was estimated at about $11,000, it being intended to build the basement first. More than the amount above was spent. After this there were many years of struggle. On account of death and removals, causing some pledges not to be paid, the church was not free of debt until 1929. Churches in Minnesota and other states benefited by the removal of about a dozen leading families, from 1920 to 1930. The Sunday school of 1907 lives in many churches.

One of the outstanding features of the days from 1908 to the early twenties was the music. The Herbert Fowler and Elias Hicks families had their own orchestra. They were real artists. The C. R. and S. C. Pew families had great music talent also. They were choir members and helped in an orchestra of a later day.

Following W. R. Burton came the ministry of C. E. Dugan and then that of William H. Knotts, known and loved in many churches. William Baier led the church for a short time and then Willard M. Leavens.

It was ultimately decided not to finish the church on Park Street, where the basement stood. The Christian Science building was offered for sale in 1937. This building was in a choice location and was in every way considered adequate to

FAIRMOUNT

the church's program; therefore it was purchased. The church paid $5,000 for the building and received $3,500 for its first location. Willard M. Leavens led the church in this transfer

Ministers since moving to the new location have been Elston E. Knight, Rodney Raymond, Orville Daemmer and Wayne Sundquist. The present minister is Howard Rosebury.

Fairmont is a county seat town. Since 1910 the population has grown from less than 2,000 to almost 10,000.

CANNON CITY AND FARIBAULT

(Rice County)

In the summer of 1869 the first sermon of the Disciples of Christ was preached in Cannon City. This is a small township, about four miles from Faribault. Mr. McElroy, the minister who preached, was visiting his daughter, Mrs. James Buchanan. These folk came from Ohio. The same year, in the fall, William Taylor remained for six weeks in the neighborhood and conducted a revival meeting for that period, after which a church was organized.

Members of that day were: John and Mary A. Bailor, Jacob and Susan Walrod, William and Jane Buchanan, David and Harriet Buchanan, James and Mary Ann Buchanan, Evaline Buchanan, Harvey Swartwoudt, Henry Swartwoudt, Rachael Swartwoudt, Sabina S. Mulliner, Sarah A. Swartwoudt, Jane Haftailen, Amanda Sanford, Catherine Swartwoudt and Emma Swartwoudt.

Cannon City was at one time a stagecoach town and it occupied a large place in the pioneer life of Minnesota. Once it came within one vote of being the county seat of Rice County. The coming of the railroads left the little township off to one side. However, the place always maintained a certain importance and the little "church by the side of the road" was one reason for that importance. It always maintained a good program with or without a minister.

The deed of this church property was recorded June 11, 1870. The trustees being Henry Swartwoudt, Sr., John Bailor and Clinton Taylor. Clinton Taylor built the church. Until it was ready, services were held in the schoolhouse, the

CANNON CITY AND FARIBAULT

Gordon Hotel and in homes of members. Among early ministers were J. C. McReynolds, J. E. Lowe and L. Y. Bailey, and two other named as Brothers Willard and Miles.

We find that the church entertained the State Convention in 1872, at the time when Brother Willard was pastor.

Ministers who held meetings or were pastors for short periods were A. P. Frost, John Truax, Henry Haggard, David Husband, W. W. Pew, J. M. Elam, T. A. Meredith and J. K. Shellenberger. David Husband organized the first Woman's Missionary Society of the Christian Woman's Board of Missions about 1896 or 1897. It was always a fine society and carried on its work until the mid nineteen-thirties.

The church was much improved in 1923, the basement made usable and sanctuary newly decorated. It was always a pleasant place and as soon as one approached it the call to worship was felt. It was, indeed, a cherished church. Your historian went out to it once each month when she was pastor-at-large for the State Board in 1911-1912.

Later helpers in the pulpit were J. H. Bicknell, C. R. Neil, C. B. Osgood, Howard Osgood, D. E. Olson, Huge Cooper, Chester Balf, G. W. Ford, Roy Ford, Harry Poll, W. D. David, W. J. Carry, James Burns and Lowell C. McPherson.

Elders who served through the years, as far as we have them, are Henry Swartwoudt, Isaac Waite, O. B. Hawley, David Buchanan, Freeman Strunk, Charles Gillham and Ralph Polson. Among the deacons were Russell Rock, James Buchanan, William Brown, Jude Hoyt, Lee Hoyt and George Buchanan.

Later young people who were of much blessing to the church were Mr. and Mrs. Arthur Nickerson, the Misses Vera and Lela Gillham and the Misses Nellie and Bernice Shultz.

Eventually the church was sold, we think in the early nineteen-forties. It was difficult to make this decision. Only a few remained, many having moved into Faribault. The church was purchased by the Nauman brothers of Cannon City, whose initials we do not know, with the promise that it would be used for community worship. These men repaired and remodeled it and we have been told that there is a resident minister and regular worship. Who shall say that the spirit of the founders has departed from this place?

FARIBAULT

(Rice County)

With the vote of the membership of the Cannon City Church the above church was started in the pleasant and important town of Faribault. Income from the Cannon City Church was put into the new building, which was a former Christian Science building. Many members were added after the move and later a parsonage was purchased. Nellie and Bernice Shultz have been great workers in Faribault as in Cannon City.

Reports are not sent from this church to the State Office, so we have no specific data; however, we have seen some of their printed material and from that we know they are working hard, striving to become a power in Faribault.

Erwin Marshall was their minister for some time. We understand that the present minister is Dean Hardy, a student of the Minnesota Bible College, who will be resident after his graduation. Their Easter program, which we saw, was an ambitious one. From that also we know they are ardent supporters of "independent" missions.

We who loved the old church pray that the spirit of loving unity, for which the Cannon City Church stood, may be again in the Faribault Church.

LITCHFIELD

(Meeker County)

The Litchfield Church fixes the date of its organization as September, 1871. The first minister came a year later. He was also the first schoolteacher in the neighborhood. Lunsford Y. Bailey was a southerner, who had fought campaigns at New Orleans and Mobile Bay. The church services were held in the log school in which Mr. Bailey taught.

Miss Nellie Minor, from whom the history was received, tells us that in this first schoolhouse an old-fashioned singing school was held. She reminds us how, around the melodeon or organ, in those days, Sunday was spent, when the whole household and friends enjoyed well-known hymns.

The church lots were given by Mr. Chauncey Butler, a wealthy banker in Litchfield. The building was donated by Mr. Ovid Butler, father of Chauncey. The edifice cost about

LITCHFIELD

$3000. It was dedicated in the early part of 1872. After the building was in use the membership was increased largely. The parsonage was built in 1883.

Early members whose names we have are: Mrs. Molly Stark Branham, Mr. and Mrs. Thomas McGannon, Mrs. Damuth, Mr. and Mrs. Timothy Jayne, Mr. and Mrs. Henry McGannon, Mr. and Mrs. Riley McGannon, Mr. and Mrs. Enoch Leavitt, Samuel Leavitt, Mr. and Mrs. S. W. Leavitt, Mr. and Mrs. N. Y. Taylor, Mr. and Mrs. E. V. Harris, Mr. and Mrs. C. T. Minor, Mr. and Mrs. J. W. Edgerly, Mr. and Mrs. A. T. Koerner, Mr. and Mrs. John Knight and daughters, Mrs. Lowater, Mrs. Belfoy, and John Shaw.

Among the first preachers were Elders Grant and Bacon and Elder H. W. Knapp. There were many periods when there was no ministerial leadership. Some of the above-mentioned church members were known to your historian in 1910 to 1920. They were people of great consecration, highly intellectual and having fine talent to give to their church. From them the Leavitts of St. Paul, Martin Minor of Minneapolis, as well as Nellie and Mattie Minor of Litchfield came. Marian and Jessie Taylor, always true to their church, are daughters of the Taylor family.

In 1884 Lewis A. Pier was minister. He started, and conducted, the *Litchfield Saturday Review* for several years. He and Mrs. Pier were greatly appreciated in the entire town. After he moved to Excelsior to become one of the faculty of Northwestern Christian College, he continued with the church as Sunday preacher.

Other ministers were P. J. Nystrom, F. E. Herthum, A. E. Major, Mr. Cohenour and Mr. E. S. Mutchler. We also find the name of Mr. Frank Leavitt. There is no full record of these ministers. We do notice that, during the ministry of Mr. Cohenour, in 1893, the Christian Endeavor State Convention was entertained in Litchfield, and that this same year dates the installation of the large art window in the front of the church.

It was in 1901 that the ministry of W. H. Knotts began. During his ministry the church was very much strengthened. It was redecorated and the colored windows put in.

LITCHFIELD

For some time after that the church was supplied for Sunday preaching from Minneapolis. Sunday school was always well planned. One outstanding superintendent was Timothy Jayne. Nellie and Mattie Minor, both public school teachers, were always faithful. There was a good Woman's Missionary Society in these earlier days, among whose leaders were Mrs. D. H. Hull, Mrs. N. Y. Taylor, Mrs. Helen McGannon and Mrs. Ina McGannon.

In 1913, the church being in need of personal evangelism, C. B. Osgood spent six weeks with them. Miss Myrtle Oliver, a teacher in the St. Cloud Normal School, helped. Following that, John Bolden was minister and during that time the mortgage on the church was paid.

In the meeting of about 1926, held by J. W. Umphries and J. Wade Seniff, other needed repairs were made on the church and E. W. Marshall became minister. He remained for about fourteen years of faithful and constructive work. Max Deweese and G. H. Cachiaras helped in evangelism during this period. Among later ministers were Frank Fleming and Alvin Nicholson.

Mr. and Mrs. W. H. Knotts have made their retirement home in Litchfield. The church very much appreciates having them in their fellowship. These servants of God will be a blessing to the community. Mrs. Knotts was present on the occasion of the 30th, the 61st and 75th anniversaries of the church. May Mr. and Mrs. Knotts spend many days in their retirement home!

MANKATO

(Blue Earth County)

We are somewhat puzzled when we read of the beginnings of the Mankato Church. We find some of the same names among the founders as those claimed by the Garden City Church. This may be part of the beautiful missionary spirit of those days. At any rate, these great Disciples seem to have been responsible for helping to found two churches, the two which have lived and worked side by side through the years.

It was organized just as Minnesota became a State of the Union, May 3, 1858. E. W. Dickinson was recognized leader of the group and chosen as elder that day. Charter members

MANKATO

named are: James B. and Elizabeth Elliott, Mrs. Clementime Elliott (mother of James B.) E. W. and Anna M. Dickinson, Marian Radford, Robert and Jessie Sharpe, Joseph and Cealy Powers, Clementine Levan, Amanda Gail Holmes, Anna Brown, Levi and Mahala Scott and Sarah Davies. The couples named together are husbands and wives. D. H. Holmes is mentioned, in 1913, as a long-time member of the church, and treasurer for twenty years. Amanda Gail became Mrs. D. H. Holmes.

Several pioneer names are among the ministers: Austin B. Council, E. T. C. Bennett, Edwin Rogers, R. W. Stevenson, David Husband, Frank H. Marshall and J. K. Shellenberger. C. B. Osgood was minister from 1909 to 1912.

The first building was dedicated in 1872. It cost $2,500. The second building, dedicated September 1, 1895, at the cost of $6,500, is the building now used. However, the property is well kept and additions have been made, so that at this date we have a structure worthy of our people in this county seat town.

We have read of Mankato of early days as being the place of a few huts, or shacks, of grass as tall as a man and of Indians lurking therein. The same year as the church was founded, the State Normal School also began. From southern Minnesota from that day students have made Mankato their educational home, and the church has been their help. In 1900 the population had grown to 10,559. One can be proud that the Disciples have been known these many years in this beautiful, and now large, city.

The membership of this church is now quoted as 208. This tells only part of the story. Mrs. Harry Hill, a daughter of Mr. and Mrs. William Shoemaker, so long servants of Christ in this church, is the wife of a California minister and mother of Homer Hill, also a minister. We can think of elders, deacons and others trained in this church and giving fine service in many places, even to the fourth generation, somewhere in the Kingdom.

Among ministers of later years have been C. W. Comstock, F. H. Groom, Enoch Gabriel, P. W. Roll, W. B. Clark, Roy Leeds, Dewey Kooy, and C. L. Duxbury. The present leader is Clyde Evans.

Pioneer preachers and wives of preachers, Minnesota (1856-1898), Mankato Convention, August 26, 1898. Left to right, front row: David Overend, Mrs. A. D. Van Dolah, John Truax. Center row: Mrs. Love A. Sandborn, Mrs. Rebecca C. Faddis, Mrs. John Truax, V. M. Sandborn. Standing: A. P. Frost, T. T. Van Dolah, and W. H. Burgess.

REDWOOD FALLS

(Redwood County)

The Redwood Falls Church has just celebrated its seventy-fifth anniversary. In 1876 Mr. and Mrs. Jesse W. Crump came to Minnesota from Louisville, Kentucky. Selling their farm, they bought property and, though they knew no other Disciples at that time, made up their minds to found their church in the new home town.

These two people sent for Elder Preston Lawton. They met in the courthouse, March 12, 1876, and organized a church with two members.

The first church was erected on a lot which they had purchased, on Third and Lincoln Streets. Mrs. Crump, herself, put all the lath on the walls in readiness for plaster. Many people, some of other churches, assisted the Crumps in building. By the time the church was one year old there were thirty members.

In 1888 the church asked the Minnesota Christian Missionary Society for help and J. G. Harrison was sent to them. On December 20, that year, thirty-three persons were organized as a church body. These members had been conducting regular Sunday services and their Thursday evening prayer meetings were attended by more people than any other service.

In 1901 there was a discussion as to whether they should repair their church building or build a new one. It was not until February, 1903, that progress was made. First, the church became a Minnesota Corporation. That year E. C. Nicholson became minister. Twelve hundred dollars was paid for the lots upon which the building now stands. It is the heart of the town, occupying a corner on an imposing square, in which the County Court House also stands. Mr. Isaac Johnson donated $1,000 of the money.

The church built was unusual in type and size, larger than many city churches. It was of Grecian design. The windows were all of beautiful stained glass, most of them presented by families or individuals. The seating capacity was for 1,000 persons. The auditorium was finished in white and gold, with light oak furnishings. This beautiful building was dedicated January 27, 1907, and in the large sanctuary there was not even standing room. The Honorable Julius Schmahl, a Minnesota jurist, was one of the speakers.

REDWOOD FALLS

The estimated figure for the building was $23,000, but the cost far exceeded that. The church was much burdened with paying the loan and church upkeep. It was not until the ministry of Oscar Joneson, in 1928, that the debt was paid, $3,520.25 being raised on one Sunday. The mortgage was burned January 6, 1929.

A great trial of faith came to this brave church only one week later, January 13, 1929—their beautiful church was burned. Christian neighbors were good. The Methodists and Presbyterians shared their buildings. A theater and the Armory were other places of meeting and the young people's work continued in the homes.

Clearing the lot began at once and by October 13, 1929, the cornerstone of the present building was laid. In it were placed a Bible, the names of the congregation, the financial statement of the church and copies of local papers. On January 20, 1930, the basement was ready for use.

The courageous minister during this time was Oscar Joneson. He was much appreciated, as was Mrs. Joneson and their sons. In May, 1937, Brother Joneson was called to his Heavenly Home. The community was saddened and the church hardly knew how to go on. For a time Mrs. Joneson led the church.

The finished building, not so large as the one preceding it, but as beautiful in its difference, was dedicated September 14, 1941, the sermon being given by F. E. Smith, secretary of the Pension Fund.

Mr. and Mrs. C. D. Clipfell began an organ fund, after the completion of the new church. Other memorial gifts were added, and finally a gift from Walter Sapp, in memory of his wife, completed the fund. In March, 1950, a concert Hammond organ was installed, and this was dedicated on June 18 of the same year.

The first minister to serve was A. P. Frost, he beginning December 10, 1876. He was followed by H. H. Abrams and T. T. Van Dolah. There were several other ministers to 1900, including Ernest Thornquist, of Northwestern Christian College. Mr. Nicholson was pastor from 1903 to 1908. Following him were Sackville M. Smith, C. F. Martin, Grover C. Schurman, J. A. Ainsworth, E. P. Gabriel, the beloved Oscar Joneson, Clyde Linsley and Harry Bucalstein. It was during the minis-

REDWOOD FALLS

try of Mr. Bucalstein that the present church building was finished. Max Randall ministered from 1945 to 1948, resigning to prepare for mission work in South Africa. Kenneth Hanson is the present minister.

The church has now a membership of 450 and the Bible school average attendance is 175. Willard Leavens, Gordon Hagberg, William McClurg, Ray Swartz and Mr. and Mrs. Lloyd Sparks are among ministers who have gone out from this church. Douglas Corpron, United Christian Missionary Society missionary, now in Yakima, Washington, was of this church. Besides the A. P. Frost family, the A. E. Major missionary family was in this church for a short time.

In later years the church has supported only "independent Missions." Their present projects are: Minnesota Bible College, Christian Home in Boise, Idaho; College of the Scripture, Louisville, Kentucky; Kaimichi Mountain Mission, Oklahoma; the Ben Allisons in the Philippines and the Morses in Tibet.

ROCHESTER

(Olmsted County)

Into this City, well known in the United States and beyond for its wonderful Mayo Clinic and associated hospitals, our church went with its ministry on July 9, 1896. Instead of beginning with a handful of members there were already about one hundred persons who put their names on the charter roll. Some of them were evidently the children of Pleasant Grove and Marion people. We will give the names we have. Mrs. Ida Brown, J. W. Flathers and family, Mr. and Mrs. E. M. Burrows, Carrie Burrows, Mr. and Mrs. Charles McLaughlin and three daughters, Della Overend, Mrs. Charles Wright and daughter, P. J. Williams, Frank Udell, Frost Parkinson, Mr. and Mrs. E. D. Fish, Ella Fish, Edna Fish, Mr. and Mrs. C. Renslow, Matt Renslow, Mrs. Martha Gates, Mrs. Emily Lamb, Mrs. Mary Vosberg, Mr. Charles Carroll, Arthur Williams and Bayard Radabaugh.

The church was organized by J. A. Erwin, State evangelist. The first minister was F. E. Utterbach.

Through the years many missionaries of our own church and other churches have worshiped with our Rochester people.

ROCHESTER

Our membership has not been large but the service given has been enormous. Until recently the minister has had a double service, that of Hospital Chaplain, as well as his pastoral and preaching duties. Only the men who have carried this task know what it has meant in long hours of work, which all of them have given so cheerfully.

The ministers, serving in turn, after Mr. Utterbach, have been C. M. McCurdy, T. T. Van Dolah, Charles W. Burridge, W. W. Devine, G. W. Wise, Rochester Irwin, C. A. Martz, B. H. Coonhardt, C. E. Burgess, R. W. Fillmore, Ernest Molloy, Loren L. De Witt, Alva T. Browning, and Dean W. Mason. The present minister is Paul G. Downs. We think the longest ministry was that of C. E. Burgess.

Having known the homes of some of our people of this church very well we can say that they all share in the hospital ministry. Many of them, as the great medical center grew, took guests into their homes. They learned how to help those whose lives grew tragic with illness. They were friends, as well as keepers of small hotels. Many gave time each week to visiting the hospitals, accepting the work planned by the church committee.

When Mr. Burgess was minister we remember one Sunday when we shared his day's work. The schedule was: Sunday school and morning worship, afternoon worship at Marion Church, two bedside communion services, Christian Endeavor and evening worship. In his long ministry, Mr. Burgess' advice was greatly prized among the churches, in the civic work of the city and in the hospital visitation. Other ministers have been so esteemed.

From the ministry of Mr. Burgess to that of Alva T. Browning there were constant efforts being made to get the help of the United Christian Missionary Society to support a minister whose sole work would be that of hospital chaplain. Other Communions had done this long before we accomplished it. However, during the ministry of Mr. Browning, help was arranged by the United Christian Missionary Society so that, with the Minnesota Christian Missionary Society, a Chaplain could be supported. E. E. Lister was called. Frequently folk write ahead to this Chaplain, who meets their trains or planes when they come to Rochester and who never leaves them alone until he sees them off on the homeward journey.

ROCHESTER

Well it is that our church serves in Rochester. The people have had their well-located building, with its beautiful sanctuary, and their membership alert at every service to seek out those who need help and fellowship. Their ministers have felt that each Lord's Day they were preaching to some whose hearts were anxious. Few churches have had so great an opportunity and none could have served with greater courage.

Recently the building has been greatly improved and enlarged. The resident membership is about three hundred. Our people are missionary minded, helping in all brotherhood enterprizes. To the young minister Paul Downs, and to the present chaplain, Vernon Carter, as well as the church, we wish many great years of service.

Alden Lee and Harry J. Hill decided to become ministers while in the Rochester church. Alden studied at Drake University and Harry at Cotner College. They are both serving in California. Homer Hill, Harry's son, is also ministering in California.

Virgil A. Sly was a member of the Rochester church when he made his decision for the ministry. For a few months he served as hospital minister. Mr. Sly commends C. E. Burgess, his pastor of those days, for the help given him in making his decision. It was about 1922 that Mr. Burgess introduced Mr. Sly in the Minnesota State Convention; we remember the event. Mr. Sly went to Cotner College that same year. Ministers and churches can live in no better way than to seek decisions for the ministry and mission field among their young people.

ST. PETER

(Nicollet County)

As early as 1858 we find mention of people of the Disciples of Christ living in Nicollet County, Mr. and Mrs. Robert Sharp, helpers in founding the churches of Mankato and Garden City among them. We have been told that Christian church members met in St. Peter and some have felt that there was an organized company. In the history of Portland Avenue Church, by David Owen Thomas, he refers to Miss Inga Lambert of St. Peter, a disciple, being married to R. T. Beebe of Minneapolis and both of them being of great service to the Portland Avenue Church.

ST. PETER

John LeGrange, mentioned in early history as a Baptist minister who helped our pioneers, lived in St. Peter. We do not know whether he ever came into that early church.

We can approximate the date of the present church in St. Peter. It was organized, under the auspices of the Southwest District in the early thirties. Cleveland church took great interest in it and some members of that church, living in St. Peter, were on its charter roll.

We visited this church about 1937 and talked to the women about organizing a woman's missionary society, since some of them had been members elsewhere. At that time they were in a small, but attractive, building of their own. They also owned a parsonage.

In parts of 1944-1945, when both Mankato and St. Peter were pastorless, Vernon S. Stagner, State Secretary, made headquarters in St. Peter, helping both churches while he looked after his executive and evangelistic tasks in the State. Most of its ministry has been supplied by the Minnesota Bible College. The longest ministry was that of W. Lloyd Hanley, a graduate Bible College student, who gave good service for four years.

WINONA

(Winona County)

Winona is an important city of southeastern Minnesota, the home of one of the State Teacher colleges. The church was organized November 10, 1901, using the following charter: "We, the undersigned believers in Jesus Christ, band ourselves together as charter members of the Christian Church in this city, the said church to have as its all-sufficient rule of faith and practice the Word of God, the Bible; and to strive in every way to follow the New Testament ideal of the Church and the Faith." Names attached: "William Baier, Mrs. William Baier, Jennie Barnes, Ira E. Berry, Mrs. Ira E. Berry, John Boetcher, Mrs. John Boetcher, Ross Bragg, Lila Duncanson, Mrs. Josephine Fort, Andrew Rouse, Mrs. Andrew Rouse, Lynn Shaffer, Edna A. Shaffer, Mollie Shaffer, J. V. Strickland, Mrs. J. V. Strickland, Henry Walworth, George P. Whitlock and Mrs. Lavinia Whitlock."

WINONA

Officers elected were: Ira Berry and John Strickland, deacons, Miss Jennie Barnes, clerk, and William Baier was asked to take care of the finances until some person should be elected for this office. These minutes were signed by William Baier. At this time Mr. and Mrs. Ira Berry are the only charter members remaining in the church. William Baier became the first regular minister.

The church grew by continual evangelistic meetings; some of the evangelists of early days were J. K. Shellenberger, the ministers of Rochester and Pleasant Grove, Rochester Irwin and M. D. Baumer, and Charles Reign Scoville.

In 1903 the church board was enlarged to three elders, four deacons, two deaconesses, clerk, treasurer and Sunday school superintendent.

In 1907 the Minnesota Christian missionary Society and the Christian Woman's Board of Missions supplied financial help for the church. C. B. Osgood was minister at that time. During his ministry, in June, 1908, the brave band of people entertained the state convention. We remember that we met in a church which must have been the Unitarian building. It was a fine convention in numbers and content.

For a time there was no building, the church having met in a Unitarian church and in a Lutheran building. On two occasions the church tried to buy the Unitarian building, but failed to make satisfactory arrangements. During 1909 and 1910 the church was homeless, but they continued to pay weekly pledges and to keep their organization as a church, pending a new location. Just previous to this, as a result of a five weeks' meeting held for the Winona churches generally, twenty-three names were give to the minister, H. D. Williams, as giving preference to the Christian church.

On September 25, 1910, through Austin J. Hollingsworth, who was acting state evangelist, negotiations were entered into with the Second Congregational Church for their building, which was offered for sale. Messrs. Berry, Freer, Haines and Jennings were the church committee. The price met was $2,700, of which a down payment of $1,000 was paid by immediate gifts of the church, the Church Extension Board helping to pay the balance. The location was West Broadway and Baker Street.

WINONA

In 1922 an extension was built on the west end of the building—two rooms and a baptistry, making added space for the church school, which was running up to 200 on occasions. George Mark Elliott was then minister. It was during this time that the church became "independent," which position it still holds.

About 1923 the Winona church led in planting the church in LaCrosse, Wisconsin. Mr. Elliott was pastor of the two churches for a while. Helping the project financially were the churches of Viroqua, Wisconsin and Huron, South Dakota.

In 1924 the church voted to have the Articles of Incorporation changed so that the church might be named "Church of Christ" instead of "Christian Church."

We find a note of the withdrawal of some of the membership in 1942. However, we do not know of any other Christian church in this city.

In March, 1944, a parsonage was purchased. The property adjoins the church. At the same time added improvements in the church property were made.

Others ministers who have served, besides those mentioned, have been: W. E. Williams, O. H. Loomis, W. L. McIllvaine, Glen R. Albro, W. D. David, J. A. Burns, L. R. Norton, E. C. Koltenbah, L. Colburn, Gus Winters, Harold Buckles, N. E. Hamilton, E. L. King, Leo Epperson. Two professors of the Minnesota Bible College have also helped on occasions—Manson E. Miller and W. E. Sperry. H. J. Frost is the present minister.

The Minnesota Christian Missionary Society servants from 1901 to 1920 had great fellowship with this church. The auxiliary society of the Christian Woman's Board of Missions was an enthusiastic one. Mrs. N. K. Flint was its president. N. K. Flint was an elder in the church. Their only son, Rex, passed away from this world in early teen age. These parents devoted money they had put aside for their son to the support of a native evangelist in our Congo Africa Mission. This lasted for some years. We prize the work of Mr. and Mrs. Ira E. Berry, faithful servants these fifty years, of the Bert Haines family, Miss Jennie Barnes, Mrs. Abel and her daughter and many others who have wrought well in their time.

Since the early twenties the church has supported only "independent" missions.

WORTHINGTON

(Nobles County)

An evangelist whose name was De Voll, from Iowa, held a meeting in Worthington in September, 1899, and at that time the church was organized. Charter members, so far as we have them, were Mr. and Mrs. G. M. Walker, Mr. and Mrs. N. H. Austin, Mrs. Francis Nichols, Mrs. John H. Holbrook and Mrs. Z. M. Smith. Mrs. John Webster, who has given us the dates of events in this church, went into its fellowship in April, 1900. Her daughter, Miss Belle Webster, has given many years of service at the Portland Avenue Church in Minneapolis.

The work grew slowly for a few years. Most of the ministry was in the hands of G. M. Walker, known as "Daddy" Walker to many in Minnesota. He gave liberally all through the years of his life.

For many years the church did not own a building. However, in 1914, the first unit of the present fine building was dedicated. It was a large tabernacle type, not intended to be permanent. The building was completed in its present form in 1923. Until 1918 Mr. Walker's leadership continued. Many evangelists helped in revival meetings.

In 1918 Mr. and Mrs. P. A. Millard went to Worthington as ministers. Mrs. Millard was a daughter of Mr. and Mrs. Walker. They were very gifted in music, both of them singers. They played many instruments. Mr. Millard was a singer of Scottish songs and a good entertainer. He was also an evangelist. He and his brother Dell, with their wives, were a well-known evangelistic team of the nineteen twenties.

When the Millards took over the ministry of the church there were forty-six members. The church now has over 500 active members. Mr. Millard served until 1941, part of the time being president of the Minnesota Bible College.

In 1934 Mr. Millard organized the Minn-Ia-Dak youth conference. About two hundred students each year, from ten to fifteen years of age, attend this conference. The meals are served in the church dining room by the Women's Council of the church. Close to Worthington there is good lake country for outings. A number of young persons of this church attended Minnesota Bible College. Some of these may be ministers but we do not have their names.

Worthington

Miss Edna M. Fellows, who ministered to the Garden City church for about fifteen years, was brought up in the Worthington church.

Following Mr. Millard, Waldo Brown ministered to the church for eight years. The present minister is Leland Patten.

Antelope Hills
(Yellow Medicine County)

This fine country church is about nine miles from the town of Canby. It stands on a hill, with its good parsonage and, like many early churches, its own cemetery. Through the years the church meeting on this hill has been a neighborly family. One has felt the peace and plenty of this fellowship.

In the home of Elder V. M. Sandborn this church was organized, August 20, 1882, with the help of Elder Truax. Charter members were: V. M. Sandborn, Love A. Sandborn, John L. Burlingame, Nancy Burlingame, Gilman Sandborn, Mary L. Sandborn, Mr. and Mrs. A. M. Morrison, Edward Todd, Mary A. Todd, Jane Todd, Jennie Todd, Jane H. Sandborn, Cora A. Sandborn, Sarah A. Doud, James M. Call, Eunice B. Call, Orrin S. Curtiss, Clista Curtiss, Lydia M. Call, Chloe L. Call, Corda E. Sandborn and Frithiof J. Kron. They organized as the Church of Christ of Antelope Hills, with V. M. Sandborn as elder, John L. Burlingame as deacon, Cora E. Sandborn as clerk, and Edward Todd, treasurer. T. T. Van Dolah was among early helpers.

The people named above were folk of great capability and many of them leaders in the State work. Until 1890 the meetings were held in the homes of the schoolhouse, which soon became entirely too small to hold the Sunday congregation. Ground on the hill was purchased in 1889 and trustees appointed to care for it and the cemetery. The church was dedicated free of debt in December, 1890, Leander Lane of St. Paul officiating.

In 1897-1898 the church was served by E. J. Sias as minister. He was a young man from Cotner College, ordained to the ministry by G. W. Elliott of South Dakota in 1898. Evangelists of early days were G. W. Elliott, J. K. Shellenberger, A. P. Frost, Brother and Sister J. A. Irwin and J. M. Elam.

ANTELOPE HILLS

Among later evangelists were J. H. Bicknell, C. B. Osgood, A. J. Hollingsworth, John G. Olmsted, M. P. Hayden and P. E. Roll.

Ministers following Mr. Sias were L. E. Scott, J. E. Hood, Lawrence Marshall and B. A. Davies, who was ordained at Antelope Hills in 1908. About 1910 Mr. and Mrs. Ole Neilsen began a long ministry, during which time the parsonage was built.

By this time many other fine families were added to the church, among them Mr. and Mrs. George A. Peterson, whose sons, Volney L. and Archie E., as well as their daughter and husband, Mr. and Mrs. George W. Maas, have been of great service. Mr. George A. Peterson was also director of the Minnesota Christian Missionary Society. George W. Maas, an elder, has also been superintendent of the Sunday school for about thirty years. With J. P. Nyquist, George A. Peterson was ordained to the eldership by evangelist S. M. Smith, in 1908.

Early visiting missionaries to the church were Adelaide Gail Frost of India and Alexander Paul and family of China. There were great workers in the Christian Woman's Board of Missions among the women of this church. Later "independent" missionaries welcomed have been the Morse family of Tibet, Mrs. Leslie Wolfe, Philippine Islands, and the Mark Maxey family of Japan.

Mrs. Josie A. Robertson, sister of George Peterson, who passed away May 30, 1949, left $2,000 to the Minnesota Christian Missionary Society and possibly $10,000 to the Minnesota Bible College.

Robert Maas, son of Mr. and Mrs. George A. Maas, is now minister of the Christian church in Buhl, Idaho.

The church was completely remodelled from 1947 to 1949. On July 24 of the latter year, Russell E. Boatman, President of Minnesota Bible College, held special services of dedication.

The membership of the church is widely scattered. In moving from the farms, some live in the towns of Canby, Madison, Dawson and Clarkfield. The Sunday school is as large as the entire resident membership. The present minister is Wesley Poll, son of Harry J. Poll. Since he is a resident minister, after a long time of student supplies, the church should go forward.

BATAVIA
(Todd County)

We write, once more, of a thriving church in the open country. White settlers came to this country about 1870.

Batavia, Browerville and Ronneby churches were organized before the turn of the century and for a long time they were our farthest north churches except Duluth.

Prior to our founding of the Batavia and Browerville churches, missionaries of the Minnesota Sunday School Union had done much evangelistic work in this section of the State. The only preaching in the Batavia section had been from these men, who also organized a Sunday school in the local schoolhouse.

The first of our ministers to visit this church were W. W. Pew, and two others mentioned as Mr. Bryant and Mr. Polly. Some people were baptized during these meetings. In 1897 the first attempt at organization was made. Several families were ready to be charter members. We cannot give the first names of many of them. There was Irene Belton, the Carry family, one of whose sons was W. J. Carry, for many years a minister; the Tyrell family, whose son, Leland, is a minister; the Hanleys, who will be better introduced in the Philbrook church; the Zappe family, whose daughter Mathilda was for many years organist in the Batavia church, and helpful in interdenominational work of Todd County, and a family named Jones. In 1929 we find a note as follows: "About two-thirds of the present resident membership is composed of members of these same families."

Lewis C. Scott ministered to the church for two years and Ira C. Smith for one year. During these three years plans were made for building, the meeting place meanwhile being the schoolhouse. Mrs. Lucy Kinney donated the lot. Much of the work of building was done by members and neighbors. In 1903, when the minister was C. N. Worden, the building was dedicated, J. K. Shellenberger preaching the sermon.

The coming of A. J. Marshall to live at the little township of Leaf River, in Wadena County, began a new day for the churches of Todd County. He preached at Batavia in 1904. He and Mrs. Marshall had been missionaries in India. Their fine family came with them, living on farms near their parents. One son, L. J. Marshall, also did some preaching and their daughter Eva was of much help to the churches.

BATAVIA

The building was destroyed by fire Sunday night, November 4, 1918. In January, 1919, C. B. Osgood and A. J. Marshall, then president of the North District, held a meeting in Batavia and planned for rebuilding. The building was completed in the summer of 1920. It cost $4,500, some of the labor being donated.

In the time when there was not a building, regular services were held; in summertime in a tent and in the winter in homes. Christian Endeavor meetings and evening services were in the regular order.

Very seldom has the church had a resident minister, particularly in later years. Sometimes it has shared ministry with Browerville, at other times with Staples. The following have served: M. P. Hayden, Sackville M. Smith (with Browerville), Robert Mueller, Hugh Cooper, W. J. Carry (with Staples), E. C. Hedlund, J. W. Caines, Emil Gustafson (with Staples), Ira Foulk and Delt Wolfe (with Staples).

Among evangelists serving were J. H. Bicknell, Hugh Cooper, C. B. Osgood and Mr. and Mrs. Lowell C. McPherson.

Since 1930 most of the ministers have been students or faculty members of the Minnesota Bible College. At the present time Manson E. Miller of the Bible College faculty is minister.

Ministers who have gone out from the church are W. J. Carry, Leland Tyrrell, Frank Paskewitz and Robert Haskins. We are not sure that the latter two are preaching now. Eliza Thorpe of this church is Mrs. Don Lawrence of Forest Lake.

The present membership is very small. The church for some years has not cooperated with the Minnesota Board or in other missionary work except the "independent" missions. The usual "open country" problem is ever present.

BROWERVILLE

(Todd County)

We have no records of the Browerville church. However, we know it was organized about 1893. There were a good church and parsonage in our early knowledge of Minnesota. We remember that in 1907 Sackville M. Smith was resident minister at Browerville and expected to minister to Ronneby also, going all the way from Todd to Benton County. He

BROWERVILLE

pleaded for the State Society to put a resident minister in
Ronneby, saying: "I cannot keep my arms around Browerville and Ronneby at the same time." In this Mr. Smith spoke
volumes. The failure of many churches in Minnesota came
because of the lack of State funds to put resident ministers
into new churches in early days of their history.

Browerville has always been a Roman Catholic stronghold
of that part of Minnesota. Due to this and to the removal of
some leading members, the work was closed much of the time
after about 1928. Some remaining members went to the
Batavia church. Mr. and Mrs. L. A. Hart, who had department stores in both Long Prairie and Browerville, closed their
store in the latter place, taking with them Mrs. Nettie Sarff,
also a valuable worker.

Eventually the state board was asked to take care of the
property which was disposed of in the early thirties.

Like that of other places, the work of Browerville must not
be forgotten.

CLEVELAND

(Le Sueur County)

The Cleveland church had its beginning at Scotch Lake, when
large groups of people were meeting in various homes for
worship.

In the fall of 1878 a meeting was held in the home of Brother
and Sister S. Rairdon, by evangelists named as Randall and
Stewart. In seventeen days of preaching, fifty-one persons made
the confessions of faith and were baptized in Scotch Lake. A
formal organization took place at this time, two elders and three
deacons being elected. On the last day of this meeting, or a
hill beside Scotch Lake, a stone foundation for the building, with
the cornerstone, was completed.

To this church, people who lived many miles away would come
for worship. We have heard that Brother Rairdon, with great
hospitality, would announce after worship that all the
FOREIGNERS were invited to his home for dinner.

In August of 1888 it was thought best to remove the building to the village of Cleveland. The structure was torn down

CLEVELAND

and the material hauled with teams. Soon after this J. K. Shellenberger, a great servant of Minnesota churches, became minister, remaining for a number of years.

An interesting document hangs in the sanctuary of the church. Headed, "COVENANT AND CHARTER MEMBERS OF THE CLEVELAND CHURCH OF CHRIST," it reads thus: "We, the undersigned, having been immersed upon our confession of faith in Christ, unite to form a Church of Christ in Cleveland, and, having already covenanted with God in Christ, do hereby covenant with each other that we will keep all the ordinances and commandments of our Lord and Saviour Jesus Christ, agreeing to be governed in our personal conduct and in our church relations and obligations by the laws of Christ as taught in the New Testament, and pledging each other to do all in our power to promote the peace, unity, and prosperity of the church, and to extend the Kingdom of Christ in all the world. In testimony we affix our respective names on this 27th day of August, A.D. 1888. Richard Randall, Henry Studley, Ancil Perkins, John Hurst, Willie Thayer, Cora E. Hurst, Charles Robinson, Mrs. H. Baker, Alice Studley, Fanny Sapp, Mrs. Frank Rohlfing, William Dickey, Lue Bartlett, Mary E. Everett, W. W. Pew, Levietor M. Pew, Charles E. Everett, Marietta Perkins, Lizzie Gilpatric, Mrs. Charles Robinson, Mrs. Fanny Rairden, Lue Studley, J. Fischer, William Lancaster, Mrs. William Dickey, Mrs. George Studley, Mattie Perkins, Lovina Hankins, Jesse Hankins, Anna Sapp, Calvin Hurst, Sam Robinson, Mrs. Sam Robinson, Mrs. George Davis, Mrs. William Davis, John Dickey, A. E. Green, Nelson Goldsmith, Sidney Rairden."

On a lot beside the church there is a parsonage, which has been used by ministers from the early years of the 20th century. Needing more room, a basement was constructed under the small building in 1924. Two years later an addition was built on the north of the church. Early in 1950 another addition, costing approximately $8,000 was completed. The minister, Marion V. Chastain, with guest ministers from Minnesota churches, led in a day of dedication of these new improvements on January 15, 1950. On this occasion it was noted that, in recent years, four members have become ministers or are giving regular Christian service, and that two are now preparing themselves at Minnesota Bible College.

CLEVELAND

The present resident membership is one hundred sixty.

From this church many families whose service has been great in Minnesota and other places have gone out. J. R. Everett and Mrs. Ethel Hurst Brandon, of Minneapolis, are among them. Elizabeth Everett (Mrs. Charles) gave great service in the Christian Woman's Board of Missions, both in Cleveland and Minneapolis.

Those now preaching or giving full-time Christian service are: E. Leo Balf, Miss Adeline Balf, Earl Grice and Mrs. Cecil Grice Scott.

COHASSET

(Itasca County)

In 1910 evangelists Austin G. Hollingsworth and John G. Olmsted held a meeting in Cohasset, after which C. E. Burgess was called as minister. This church was a project of the Minnesota Christian Missionary Society, with American Christian Missionary Society help.

Charter members whose names we have are: Mr. and Mrs. Will Wood, Mrs. F. O. Boggs, R. K. Stokes, Mr. and Mrs. Guy Wood, Mr. and Mrs. Glen Wood, Mr. and Mrs. Frank Wood, Mrs. William Smith, Mrs. Dickey, Mr. and Mrs. F. W. Stockwell, Mr. and Mrs. Cleveland, Edward Curtiss, Mr. and Mrs. Sam Combs, Mr. A. R. Bullock and Mr. and Mrs. Edward Dibley. Mrs. R. K. Stokes came to the church soon after and she has been a devoted leader.

A congregation of about forty-four used a hall, over offices, as their first meeting place. They could have had no better pastor than the versatile C. E. Burgess as their leader. In him they had a highly educated man, a great leader and preacher and, most of all, a man who could well understand folk of a new and growing country town. Mr. Burgess loved Itasca County, with all its beauty. He has been known since as minister of our churches in Rochester, Minnesota, Boise, Idaho, and Honolulu, Hawaii.

The first deacons were Glen, Guy and Frank Wood. The elders were Will Wood and Edward Curtiss.

About 1914 the church was able to purchase a schoolhouse. This was a good building and served well for many years as the meeting place for the growing congregation. At times

COHASSET

there have been pastorless periods and also student preachers for Sunday only, but the church has been served well by its officers, who have kept all the regular services going.

We cannot give a full list of ministers who served in the "schoolhouse" days. Among them were Elmer Hedlund and Eldon Chitwood. Ronald F. Keeler, professor of the Minnesota Bible College, did Sunday supply and also summer resident work.

In 1939 the church realized its dream of having their new church building. This was a great lift to the membership. Just now they are enlarging the building and expect to dedicate the whole soon.

The church is in excellent condition. The minister, E. C. Steffy, is a fine leader. There are 150 active members of the church and the Sunday school enrollment is 200.

CONCORD

(Dodge County)

One rides out about five miles from the railroad town of West Concord to "Old Concord," as it is often called. The old town became a settlement in early Minnesota days. It is a peaceful spot, a neighborly place, and our church is one of the "wildwood" type. In visits between 1910 and 1915, we have seen sleds drive up to the church on Sunday evening and, cold notwithstanding, the house filled with worshipers.

The congregation was first organized, possibly by David M. Haggard, in 1858. Charter members were: David M. Haggard, Mary A. Haggard, Benjamin Woodward, Hannah Woodward, Reeding Woodward, Levi P. Hill, Christina Hill, Thomas B. Haggard, Ebenezer Tilden and Elizabeth Tunks. The officers of the organization were David M. Haggard, elder and Levi P. Hill, deacon.

Among those who preached in early days were B. U. Watkins, John Truax, Charles Levan and A. J. Rutan. Doubtless most of the pioneer evangelists were, at some time, giving service in this church. Few of the churches had pastoral service full time. A. P. Frost ministered to this church at the time when his daughter, Adelaide Gail Frost, later missionary to India, was baptized.

CONCORD

Perhaps, like other churches, there was rather spasmodic work in early days. The church must have met in homes and such public buildings as were available. The building was dedicated in 1878; it cost something over $2,500.

Two men who are specially mentioned by the church for their services are Milbird Wray and William C. Tibbets. The former served for fifty years, the latter for thirty. They are spoken of as "men above reproach, full of the Holy Spirit and faith."

The son of Milbird Wray was an ardent worker in the Grand Avenue Church in Minneapolis and Milbird's grandchildren, Ross and Robin Wray and Nola (Mrs. Wallace Schorr) served in both Grand Avenue and Lake Harriet churches. Also Violet Wray Brace (Mrs. Clayton Brace) in Grand Avenue and Central church, Denver, Colorado.

The grandfather of Alden Lee and Harry J. Hill, ministers in California, who was a village blacksmith and elder of a pioneer group meeting in Oronoco, baptized Mrs. Milbird Wray in Concord Creek.

Dr. Bently Ray served for some years as pastor of the Concord church. One of his sons is a trusted officer in the First Church in St. Paul.

An unusual character in the Concord church was "Uncle" Christ Sprighter. We remember him especially for his kindly hospitality and his keen interest in the work of the State, shown by his frequent visits to the state office. Nancy Jane Haggard, eldest child of David Haggard, also was in the church. She lived to be more than 100 years old.

The church of today seems to be rather small and we are unable to find much news of later years. Perhaps the usual open country problem accounts for this. We feel sure, however, that Sunday school and preaching, when possible are still held in the building at "Old Town," as Concord is frequently called.

EAGLE LAKE

(Blue Earth County)

Another Blue Earth County church is Eagle Lake, which was founded in 1856 by two families, named Burgess and Braden, who came to that county by covered wagon from Indiana. The

EAGLE LAKE

meetings were in the Burgess' home, then later held in a log schoolhouse. In 1879 the present building was erected. From Mr. II. A. Fuller of Wauwatosa, Wisconsin, we have heard that William Burgess was minister in Eagle Lake about 1891. The church had a thriving organization at that time. Soon after that Frank H. Marshall preached each Sunday afternoon. Most of the time ministry has been sustained on a part-time basis. About 1908 Leland Porter ministered to both Cleveland and Eagle Lake.

We read of many meetings being held in this church and such evangelistic names as David Husband and Mr. and Mrs. J. A. Erwin. We also find a note of an evangelist named Childs, perhaps the same J. P. Childs who preached in Fairmont about 1906. The church then was evidently strengthened and had full-time preaching.

The church has endeavored to keep its Sunday school and worship through the years. At present Miss Burnette Neville is minister.

FOREST LAKE

(Washington County)

We remember very well the beginnings of the Forest Lake Church, when Harland Swanson wrote to fellow churches in Minnesota, asking that they sell "bricks" for the proposed Forest Lake Church. We also heard Mr. Swanson speak in state conventions of the project so near to his heart. Meantime, services were being held in a schoolhouse. A meeting was held by Mr. Stein during these days.

The organization date was October 9, 1909. The first building was a tabernacle. J. H. Bicknell held a fruitful meeting for the church while they were in this building. However, the permanent building was dedicated on November 20, 1910. John G. Slater, minister of the Portland Avenue Church, Minneapolis, preached the dedicatory sermon. Austin J. Hollingsworth and J. G. Olmsted held a meeting that same autumn.

Richard Dobson, a minister who was at that time keeping a local hotel, became pastor. Other ministers who served were P. N. Nystrom, George Rossman, Hugh Cooper, C. H. Durose,

FOREST LAKE

J. L. McBean, G. H. Cachiaras, Frank Paskewitz, G. V. Ferguson, Noah Garwick, Perry Baldwin, Virgil Frederick, Harold McFarland and H. H. Webster. Most of these were either students or other nonresident men.

Forest Lake is a beautiful town in the playground, lake district, near the Twin Cities. Many summer tourists visit this section, of which the little town is the chief business center. It is an excellent farming community. Many fine Scandinavian folk are among the farmers.

A church in such a place must needs outgrow its building. In 1917 a two-story, six-room building was added for Sunday school and social purposes. We think this was done in the time of Hugh Cooper's ministry. The beautiful parsonage was dedicated June 8, 1930.

The present minister, Don A. Lawrence, began his work April 16, 1939. He is a graduate of the Minnesota Bible College and no man could fill a town church, with large rural membership, better than he. Mr. and Mrs. Lawrence are outstanding in pastoral work and one would never tire of listening to Don preach. The church is unique in having a school bus, which brings in people each Sunday for Bible school and worship. A double garage was built in the fall of 1939, to house the minister's car and the bus.

The building was badly damaged by fire December 20, 1942. Some of the two-story building remained. The church at once planned to rebuild, of course better than before. October 24, 1943, the new building was dedicated. Your historian was happy to be in this service. Forrest L. Richeson preached the sermon.

The Holmquist family were charter members. Fred Holmquist and other members of this family have been leaders in music from the first days of the church.

There are one hundred sixty resident members today. With Mr. Lawrence's consecrated ministry there should be further growth. Mrs. Don Lawrence before her marriage was Eliza Thorpe and belonged to our Batavia church. She and their daughters have been especially fine helpers in Mr. Lawrence's work, both at Audobon Park, Minneapolis, and at Forest Lake.

GARDEN CITY
(Blue Earth County)

Quoting from the Garden City church history, given at the 75th anniversary in 1933, we read of the pioneer days: "There were no telephones, no electric lights, no railroads, no automobiles, no airplanes, no gravelled or paved roads. . . . There were no churches, few schools, and religious services were held in the homes."

Robert Sharp and Williston K. Greenwood were the first two men whose faithfulness led to the organization of the church. The former lived in Nicollet County, nine miles west of Mankato. He was a great student of the Bible and a clear thinker. He and Mrs. Sharp were Scottish people, having come from the land of the "Banks and Braes" soon after their marriage. The latter located on a farm on the Watonwan River, about five miles from Garden City. Mr. Greenwood knew of Mr. Sharp's ability to preach, and invited him to come and help organize a church in his home. Mr. Sharp walked twenty-four miles each way and, during that summer of 1858, made the journey frequently to preach for the little church.

Those who banded themselves together, in order to teach their neighbors and friends, were the two families named, and Levi and Mahala Scott. They faithfully met at the Lord's Table and the fellowship meant much in their lives. The meetings were usually at the Williston K. Greenwood farm. By July 10, 1859, a few more Disciples were found and added to the group.

The first baptism in this part of the country was performed by H. Burgess, pastor at Livola. It was that of Amanda Gail, who afterward was Mrs. D. N. Holmes, a faithful member of the Mankato church. It was for her that Adelaide Gail Frost was named. This baptism was performed in the evening, in the Watonwan River, by the light of prairie fires.

The brethren heard of Elder Charles Levan, who was holding a meeting in St. Peter. They called him, and he led a meeting for them beginning February, 1860. This resulted in a number of additions. Sometimes in store buildings, and more often in homes, the people continued to meet.

About 1860 the brethren of Belle Plaine, Le Sueur, St. Peter and Garden City formed a cooperative society for evangelism

GARDEN CITY

and employed Dr. Robert Rutan as evangelist. This society seems to have been the parent of the Minnesota Christian Missionary Society.

The fall of 1862 saw the uprisings of the Indians. Some folk had to leave their homes, as recorded in the preface of this book. Until the spring of 1863 there were no meetings, although the Lord's Supper was observed. There was no regular preaching until the fall of 1864, when A. P. Frost, one of the state evangelists, visited them. They then resumed their public services in Watonwan schoolhouse. Due to hardship and other drawbacks which new settlers had to endure, sometimes only five or six people were present at services, and the sisters would give thanks for the Bread and Cup when there were no male members who felt they could do so. Williston K. Greenwood was recognized as their overseer, or elder.

It was not until 1878 that any real organization was attempted. Then Leonard C. Schumaker was chosen as elder and J. K. Greenwood and C. H. Bland as deacons. There were seventeen members. During the next years 13 more were added and nine more up to 1882.

We find no other records until 1888, when a band of about 25 members was meeting in a Baptist church, with Edwin Rogers as pastor. After that services were held in a hall and, in the winter of 1889, R. W. Stevenson, who was preaching in Mankato, held a revival meeting which resulted in about forty being added to the church. With this new strength the church called John Truax to be minister in December, 1889. During his ministry the lot on which the church now stands was purchased.

It was on May 1, 1892, that the house of worship was dedicated, with Lewis Pier of Excelsior and David Husband of Mankato officiating. Following that, in their turn, S. S. Phillips, Frank H. Marshall and Claire L. Waite were ministers. Then, in 1896, the J. A. Erwins led in a meeting, during which many more were added to the church.

Other ministers serving to 1906 were W. H. Rust, C. L. McIntyre, J. F. Ainsworth, J. E. Hood and Bruce Black.

The church by this time had gathered strength and kept on in a fine, faithful, missionary way, having regular ministry.

GARDEN CITY

During the ministry of Frank Forster, Ada L. Forster was ordained to the ministry, in 1907. Another ordination was that of John G. Olmsted, in 1912, at which time he became their minister, remaining until 1918. It is interesting to note that Mr. Olmsted married Miss Susie Mills, in 1910, and their son is Gilford E. Olmsted, former pastor of the Sioux Falls church, South Dakota, and now field representative for Drake Bible College.

We should mention that, from early settlers, the Lucius and Fillmore Mills families have been among the most staunch members of the church and have been leaders worthy of the founders, Mrs. Fillmore Mills being a daughter of Mr. and Mrs. Robert Sharp.

Six students of Northwestern Christian College are listed as of Garden City, proving the desire of the church to train people for Christian work. Maud Waite Marshall (Mrs. Frank H.) was of this church.

The first addition to the church building was made during the ministry of Edna M. Fellows, which began in May, 1923. Miss Fellows' first pastorate was of ten years, and she returned after an illness for a second pastorate of five years. Miss Fellows was a trained worker among young people and children. It was necessary to add two rooms for the Sunday school, these being dedicated in October, 1925. During Miss Fellows' second pastorate a parsonage was left to the church by the John Osgood family. Mr. and Mrs. Osgood were among the very faithful members of the church. So many others ought to be mentioned, both ministers and laymen, but we include all of them when we say that the work of the years has made Garden City the most outstanding town church in Minnesota, especially in their missionary giving.

The ministry of Clyde Leeds, concluded in 1950, was one of almost ten years. During his time the "God's Portion" plan was started. Each year the church brings an offering, over and above all other offerings. The money is used for local and missionary work. Men, women, boys and girls bring whatever they have earned from whatever they set aside for "God's Portion" during the year. The day of giving means a great lift, spiritually and financially, to the church.

Like every small town church Garden City has given its members, over and over again, to the cities. Today, with a

GARDEN CITY

resident membership of 169, the missionary giving from July, 1949, to June, 1950, was $3,144.92, an average of 18.61 per member. Their buildings are kept in tip-top shape and their local program fills most of their church space each Sunday.

This church has provided officers and members of the Minnesota Christian Missionary Society from both its ministers and laymen. Mr. and Mrs. Henry Esch are the consecrated leaders of the church today.

This pleasant town and countryside has but two churches, the Baptist church, the first to be built, and the Christian church. There was, for some years, a Methodist church. When services were discontinued almost all of the members left, transferred their membership to the Christian church. These members have been of great help through the years. Other members serving this church have been F. H. Stringham, R. B. Jones and the much honored and beloved Richard Dobson.

HORICON

(Martin County)

Situated between Truman and Fairmont, a quiet spot in the open country, is the Horicon church, a little white church, with its cemetery adjoining. Through the years this church has become a beloved spot to many families of the farming community. Frequently this church has been ministered to jointly with Truman. We understand that, at the present time, the church lives entirely independent of other churches of Minnesota, but that it does have ministry.

A Sunday school was organized prior to 1893 in this community. Some of the leaders being Congregationalists. One cannot but believe that earlier than this some attempts for church life had been made; the region was settled earlier than the coming of our evangelists.

In 1893 W. O. King held an evangelistic meeting. He was followed by David Husband, State evangelist, supported in part by the Christian Woman's Board of Missions. The church was organized in 1894. That year the building was erected by Charles Popple of Fairmont. There were fifty-two members.

We do not have the names of the charter members. However, we remember that a number of people who afterward belonged to the Fairmont church were baptized, due to the work of this

HORICAN

church; members of the George S. Fowler family, the P. S. Hicks family and others. Mrs. Mary Sargent and her daughter, Mrs. Evans, were ardent workers in the Horicon church, also the Reeder and Greeley families and Mr. and Mrs. J. E. Salisbury, in the early days of the church. The Holmes Fowler family (not related to the former Fowlers) was also of the little company. We wish a larger list might be available. As we remember these people, they are ardent lovers of their church and believed in its opportunities.

Alden Lee Hill ministered to Truman and Horicon in 1907. In 1911, Mr. and Mrs. W. O. King returned to the Horicon pastorate, remaining until 1918, giving full time. Ole Neilsen ministered to this church about 1924-1926. Students of the Minnesota Bible College frequently have given Sunday preaching.

For some time the church has been interested in, and supported, the work of Benjamin F. and Edith Wolfe Allison in the Philippine Islands. Mr. Allison was their minister for a short time.

HOWARD LAKE

(Wright County)

The Howard Lake church was organized in 1872. We have no list of charter members. M. C. Rickerson gave the lot and helped to build with his own hands.

The little town is situated on a beautiful lake, for which it is named. While it is in the summer resort section it has an urban atmosphere, with its good business section and offices of professional men. Through the years the church has opened its doors to many visitors and provided for them real, spiritual worship.

Highly intellectual people, well versed in the message of the Disciples of Christ, had leadership in this church. We regret not having a full list. We think of Mrs. E. LaDow, mentioned in our "Historical Personalities"; her daughter, Mrs. F. E. Latham, and the family of the latter; also Mrs. C. M. Chilton and her family. Children of these families were students at the Northwestern Christian College. Fay Latham Porter is now a worker in the Portland Avenue Church, Minneapolis. Other devoted members were Mrs. Sallie E. Thompson, Mr. and

HOWARD LAKE

Mrs. John Mealey, Mrs. Minnie Headley, Mrs. A. Kemper and
two daughters, and Mr. and Mrs. E. C. Tuttle, whose daughter,
Lorna Mae, has been for many years a leader in the Young
Woman's Christian Association, and who is now the chief
executive in the Denver, Colorado, branch.

Two ministers came from this church, Ernest Molloy, of
Deep River, Iowa, and Erwin Marshall, pastor of the Plainview
Church, Minnesota.

Among ministers giving service through the years were J.
C. McReynolds, George Bacon, James Denton, E. Pierce, L. Y.
Bailey, David Campbell, John Truax, John Grice, Lee Ferguson, William H. Knotts and Leland W. Porter. It was
during the fruitful ministry of Mr. Knotts that the church was
remodeled and the baptistry and pews installed.

The present minister is G. H. Cachiaras, Dean of the Minnesota Bible College. He has served for almost twenty-eight
years. During this time the church has been moved back
forty feet from the street. New basement, ceiling and new
furniture have been added. Pastor Cachiaras is very much
appreciated in the church and community.

KIMBALL

(Stearns County)

A history, compiled for the 75th anniversary of the Kimball
churches, dates the beginning of the work of Maine Prairie in
1862. We quote from that history to show the inflow of people,
some of whom made our churches. "Eighteen-fifty-six and fifty-
seven were boom years in Minnesota. Many thousands of
splendid men and women poured into the new territory from
comfortable homes back east, hoping to find richer and better
homes for their children. Some of them wanted to get rich
quickly, so they would pre-empt or buy one hundred sixty
acres of land, lay out a town site on their place and send copies
back east, expecting their friends to buy the lots. They were
called 'paper town sites,' but they did not always pan out."

One such man, a Mr. Cutter, built a fine home on Pearl
Lake, a great contrast to the log homes of others. His lots not
selling, he was obliged to let his home go. B. U. Watkins, of
Indiana, bought this home. He was highly educated, a scholar

KIMBALL

of Hebrew, Greek and Latin. Two young men, D. E. Meyers and Alva P. Frost, studied Greek with him. Each married one of his daughters. D. E. Meyers was later superintendent of St. Cloud Reformatory and Alva P. Frost a Christian minister.

It might also be mentioned here that one of the industrial factories of Minnesota came from this family. Elder Watkins' son, J. E., started making liniment in the attic of his father's home. This led to the Watkins' Medicine Factory in Winona. This Mr. Watkins later had no church connection of which we know, but we have heard on good authority that he, at one time, was giving twenty widows of ministers each $25 a month for as long as they lived. The factory still continues.

In 1863 Elder Watkins preached in a log schoolhouse, built that year. This was the first preaching on Maine Prairie. People came from miles around and the preaching time was frequently the only occasion upon which the far-scattered people would see each other. Sometimes a member would take the whole congregation home to dinner. These were great occasions. Later D. B. Stanley built a store on Maine Prairie Corners, with a hall above it. Here Elder Watkins continued the church and Sunday school gatherings.

The American Christian Missionary Society, about that time, sent Emerson Van Dervort as missionary to the state of Minnesota. He settled in the Maine Prairie section, but helped in many meetings in the surrounding country. His nephew, A. W. Van Dervort, afterward became minister of Minnehaha Church, Minneapolis.

It was in Stanley Hall, February 9, 1870, that the Maine Prairie church was organized, in the presence of J. J. Parker of Clearwater, Elder Watkins giving the sermon of the day. Charter members were Datus E. Meyers, David B. Stanley, Thomas B. Stanley, T. J. Wiley, B. U. Watkins, Henry Wiley, Orlinda Wiley, Samaria Barrett and Mary Stanley. We also read of this date: "Elder Watkins lost his wife in 1870 and went back to Indiana in 1871." Another note, dated April 9, 1871, says: "The congregation being without an elder, we proceeded to elect by vote two elders, Abraham Shoemaker and George Green. D. S. Stanley was elected clerk and E. C. Bennett treasurer." At this time there were forty-five mem-

bers. Elder Shoemaker was a man of friendly qualities and
he gave great leadership, as did Elder Watkins.

We find, about 1887-1888 that John Truax preached at Fair
Haven, Maine Prairie and Eden Valley, sections of the country
close together; also that W. W. Pew was called in 1889 to
preach for Eden Valley and Maine Prairie. He was to receive
$250 a year from Maine Prairie and the record runs: "He
was the first minister to draw a salary."

It was not until 1890 that the Maine Prairie church was
built. It was dedicated in October of that year.

The church had grown by this time. Two of Abraham
Shoemaker's sons C. D. and Merrit and their wives and families were giving fine leadership. We think of Mrs. I. E. Met-
calf among the women, and Dr. and Mrs. George Sherwood's
faithful service.

On May 11, 1915, the church was moved from Maine Prairie
to the town of Kimball. Having been altered from time to
time, in order to make more room, as well as more comfort and
beauty, we find a good plant today, as the result of the work of
the founders.

Some of the ministers since 1900 have been W. H. Knotts,
Hugh Cooper, Dr. R. Bentley Ray, Waldo Brown, Erwin
Marshall and Kenneth Brooks. The present minister is Ellis
Beeman.

LAMBERTON

(Redwood County)

The small church of this town, not far from Redwood Falls,
was organized by the Southwest District in the early nineteen-
twenties. A building was purchased. Your historian visited
the church on two occasions in 1923-1924, at which time there
seemed to be a good future for this work. Enoch Gabriel, when
he was minister at Redwood Falls, did most of the work of organization and gave fine oversight to the church. We seem to
remember that John Gabriel, brother of Enoch, also gave some
leadership.

A number of ministers have served this church for short
periods. The present minister is listed as Norville Tolle and
the membership is estimated by the state office as seventy-five.

LEAF RIVER

(Wadena County)

The little community church in this township had good fellowship with the Todd County churches while Mr. and Mrs. A. J. Marshall ministered there. The church was of many denominations. During the Marshalls' stay they often studied our world missions and gave to them. They attended our District conventions and state workers often enjoyed visiting with them and addressing them. We think the Marshalls left there in the middle nineteen-twenties.

LEWISVILLE

(Watonwan County)

This church must needs claim the same origin as Madelia. There were those who remained in the Antrim church for a few years after the Madelia church was started. Soon after, however, the Antrim building was moved to Lewisville and placed on a corner lot in that village.

At this time Elder Robert Dewar was the recognized leader and perhaps the greatest period of service was early in the twentieth century. Robert Dewar's brother and sons of both of them were active in the church.

For many years, even after the church did not have a minister, the Woman's Missionary Society was active. Among the leaders were Mrs. Robert Dewar and her daughter, Mrs. Libbie Lewis. Many women of the village who had no connection with the church were in the missionary society. Miss Bertha Davies and her brother Mark were valuable younger helpers of that day.

Ministers of the Madelia church frequently served Lewisville. However, we find that sometimes the latter church was associated with Willow Creek, as was the case early in its history, when Leslie Wolfe, afterward a missionary to the Philippines, served both these churches.

A period of prosperity is to be noted about 1918, when in the ministry of Emil Gustafson the church building was raised and a basement built, and many improvements made in the upper structure.

Removals of members to other places weakened the work, but those going out carried on in other churches, notably Madelia, Truman and Fairmont.

LEWISVILLE

ˋAlmost all State evangelists and secretaries helped at some time in this work, until the late thirties, when practically no regular services were held. We believe the building still remains and the state office gives an estimate of about twenty members in the town.

Harry Poll, minister, and Mrs. Poll were members of the Lewisville church, also Arthur Poll, now minister in Minneapolis.

MADELIA

(Watonwan County)

Madelia is another thriving town, the business place for a large farming district.

We date back to 1877 for the foundation of this church. Mr. Archibald A. Law, a farmer living about two miles from Madelia, organized a church in Antrim township and served as its pastor, without salary. The farm of this good man is still known as the "Law Farm." We might mention here that Mrs. Chester Pew, a charter member of the Fairmont church, was a daughter of Mr. Law and that others of the same family helped in churches in Minnesota. We have no membership list of the 1877 organization.

In the summer of 1895 David Husband held a meeting in the Antrim church and arranged for them to cooperate with some members in Madelia, for the purpose of supporting a minister for the two places. Thus, on November 1, 1895, J. K. Shellenberger moved to Madelia and held church services in the upper room of a schoolhouse. That Mr. Shellenberger was a blessing to many churches can easily be seen by this history.

On March 9, 1896, Mr. Shellenberger began a protracted meeting, assisted by R. A. Givens as singer. In those days such meetings often lasted over five Sundays. The audience grew too large for the room mentioned and the Baptist brethren gave an invitation for the meeting to occupy that church. This was accepted. The results were that fifty people were baptized and nineteen came by statement.

We would like to quote from early information sent to us by Mrs. Joseph Davies: "Churches of this communion are under a strict congregational government and recognize no

MADELIA

supervising authority other than the New Testament. The terms Christian church, Churches of Christ and Disciples of Christ are practically interchangeable."

The first church organization in Madelia was made April 12, 1896, electing C. L. Young, Samuel Etter, C. R. Pew and William Johnson as deacons. Also a Sunday school was organized with the pastor as superintendent, Mrs. William Johnson as assistant superintendent, Maud Donley, secretary, and Mrs. W. G. Wicks, treasurer.

On July 4 of the same year three trustees were elected: Thomas Donley, J. Travis and Chester Pew, and on September 10th of that year the site upon which the church building now stands was selected. A building committee, the minister, D. A. Babcock and C. L. Young were also appointed. These men brought plans on September 24, which were accepted and the committee authorized to proceed with the building.

In December, 1896, the building was completed. The cost was $4,000. Thus so swiftly, in this eventful year, the Madelia church started its long and faithful journey.

Charter members of the church are given as: Mr. and Mrs. J. K. Shellenberger, Thomas Donley, Mary Donley, Samuel Etter, Minnie Etter, Martin Etter, Caroline McIndoo, C. R. Pew, Mrs. C. R. Pew, John Travis, William Johnson, Mrs. William Johnson, Esther Young, Anna McIndoo, Richard Young, C. L. Young, Mrs. Martin Etter, D. A. Babcock, Frank Rairdon, Louida M. Pew, A. J. McLean, M. V. Tackels, Mrs. M. V. Tackels, Mrs. John Scott, Mrs. E. M. Wallace and W. L. Hackney.

For many years the church cooperated with the Antrim and Lewisville churches for ministry. (Antrim was moved to Lewisville about the turn of the century.) Most of the ministers resided in Madelia.

Succeeding Mr. Shellenberger were J. Crock, J. C. Radford, John Harris, George Brown, F. A. Stringham, Burton Hoffman, John McKee, Emil Gustafson and Jack Caines. At this point some of the ministers were students and they ministered to Madelia alone. They were Edwin Root, P. E. Poll, Roland Wilder, LeRoy Crocker, Clarence Potter, Mark Maxey and Dean Orris. Roland Wilder, who lives on a farm near

MADELIA

St. James, is the present minister. This is his second pastorate with the church. He is the son of E. P. Wilder of the Willow Creek church.

This hospitable church has often entertained State workers and for many years shared in state and national missionary effort. We would look back to fellowship with Mr. and Mrs. Joseph Davis, Mrs. John Scott, the H. P. Leonard family and others who were such fine missionary workers of that day.

We close with a prayer that the future of the church may mark new ways of faith.

MARION

(Olmsted County)

On another beautiful spot, for many years, there has stood the little church called "Marion." Had it not been for some folk choosing to make Pleasant Grove their church home, this might easily have been the first church to be organized in Minnesota. It was in 1866 that T. T. Van Dolah, perhaps at that time he was minister at Pleasant Grove, organized the Marion church. As we look over the names of the charter members, we feel that there must have been others. We have Mr. and Mrs. Thomas Bonham, Mr. and Mrs. Charles Perry, Mr. and Mrs. Skeels, and Mrs. Julia Poter (perhaps the latter should be Porter). In later days this church, too, has shared the fate of many open country churches. Though smaller, it still holds services.

The building was erected in 1872. Frequently the minister of the Rochester church has held afternoon services at Marion.

We remember many times when this hospitable church has been host to district conventions. It must have been that in early days state conventions were held there, too. This church, also, was very missionary. A woman known over all the State for her earnest work, at the turn of the century and afterward, was Mrs. Persis Nickum. Her brother Seth Mc-Caleb and his wife and family were tireless workers.

We think of Lily Predmore and her sisters. These folk were eager for higher education. Lily studied at Cotner College and gave great service in the Sunday school of her home church. Her sisters, business girls, also gave much help in the

MARION

Sunday school and young people's work. Luella McCaleb, sister of Seth and Mrs. Persis Nickum, studied at Northwestern Christian College and Drake University and married William John Minges, a well-known evangelist from 1910. Together they served for some years in this field and afterward, for seventeen years, they were leaders of the West Palm Beach Church, Florida. Another of this family, Cora E. McCaleb, also studied at Drake University and became the wife of a minister, R. H. Heicke, giving many years of service with him. Then there were Mrs. Bragg and her fine daughters. One of them, Ethel, moved to Des Moines and gave her service in the University Place Church. We have heard that a son of Seth McCaleb was a student of the Minnesota Bible College.

Changes there have been, but today the doors of the old Marion church are still open each Sunday for worship. The "Witnesses," living and dead, continue the glorious work founded almost eight-five years ago.

MELVIN

(Polk County)

Hugh Cooper, C. B. Osgood and others led in helping the people who lived near the little village of Melvin to organize a church. There were just a few families and, as we remember, the D. Holmes family were among the leaders in this work. It lasted but a short time, but we recall the good fellowship we enjoyed in visiting the church. Some of its members moved to Washington State and carried on their work there. These people were fine Christians and, had they stayed, we believe the Melvin church would have prospered.

NEVIS

(Hubbard County)

About 1902-1904 the Baptist people began to build in this small town, in the northern lake country of Minnesota. This is another town in the midst of the holiday country, where winters are hard, but summers see many visitors coming into town for worship. Some well-known ministers and college leaders have preached in this little church.

NEVIS

Before the Baptist building was finished they asked persons who had belonged to the Christian church elsewhere to help them, with the understanding that both groups could use the church when finished.

A. J. Marshall, so useful for many years in the North District, gave the church much help and advice, as well as preaching. Ultimately, the Christian church group grew to be the larger. They bought out the financial interest of the Baptist people in the building and organized their church in 1908.

Among those who started the work were Mr. and Mrs. William Cary, their sons, Other and Frank Cary and the families of each of them. Mr. Dan Cornwall, who gave us part of this record, joined soon after, having been a member of other Christian churches in Minnesota and North Dakota. Mrs. Otto Johnson, so useful in Audubon Park Church, Minneapolis, was formerly of Nevis church.

The church has never been able to carry a large program and often the members have been obliged to keep up their services without a minister. Leaders now are Mrs. Bert Davis, Mrs. Harry Dillon, Mrs. James Shortridge and Mr. Ross Scott.

Many times, from 1910 to 1920, this church has entertained the North District convention and always it has seemed like a vacation for those attending, so beautiful was this place in early fall.

The building was improved in 1921, making a good plant for all activities. Students of the college have also preached for the church in recent years. The state office estimates the membership as one hundred and the resident minister named is Loren Emerson.

PHILBROOK

(Todd County)

The little village of Philbrook is on the main line of the Northern Pacific Railroad, not many miles from Staples, which is a railroad center. It is only about seven miles from the Batavia church.

Thinking that there should be a church in this town, Mr. and Mrs. Chester Hanley and some others were led by A. J. Marshall to organize. We have not been able to get the date of the

PHILBROOK

building, which is a very neat structure in the center of the village, but we know the church was part of the Minnesota fellowship prior to 1920.

The membership was never large. There were few times when a resident minister could be maintained. One serving loyally was William Yarlett and his wife. They had been in Salvation Army service and they were devoted Christian people. Mr. Yarlett contracted tuberculosis in the first World War and died in the Veterans' hospital in Minneapolis in June, 1948. Mrs. Yarlett was minister of our church in Chippewa Falls, Wisconsin, for some years. Mr. and Mrs. Yarlett also served at Ronneby.

Mr. and Mrs. Chester Hanley, Miss Irene Belton and others were among those who led this church. Mrs. Hanley led in a Woman's Missionary Society. She also served on the state board. Their son, Lloyd, attended the Minnesota Bible College and is now minister at Fort Benton, Montana. He and his wife (also a Philbrook girl) have done much in evangelistic singing. More than to any others, the church owes its life to the Hanley family. Mrs. Hanley is a sister of the minister W. J. Cary.

The church no longer sends reports, but the state office estimates their membership at 25. Manson E. Miller supplies them with Sunday preaching, as he does Batavia. They also have Sunday school.

PLAINVIEW

(Wabasha County)

This church of early Minnesota history was organized by Abraham Shoemaker in 1861. There were twelve charter members, whose names we do not have. We think one of them was the clerk of 1913, Mrs. E. M. Bates, who wrote a history for the state office that year.

Services were first held in Wilcox Hall and then in the first Plainview schoolhouse. The latter was purchased by the congregation and moved to a lot which the railroad later bought. The building was then moved again to lots on which the present church now stands.

In 1895 it was voted by the congregation to build a new church home, at a cost not to exceed $3,000. When the allotted

amount was found to be increased by $650, the old building
and one of the lots were sold. On January 7, 1902, the church
was freed of debt, largely by the persistence of the Women's
Society of the church. The minister during this time was C.
W. Martz, and says the record, to this faithful leadership,
largely, was the success of the building.

Mentioned as early ministers are B. U. Watkins, Alva P.
Frost, T. T. Van Dolah, H. D. Williams, F. E. Utterback,
Ernest Thornquist, and after the turn of the century G. W. Wise
and J. M. Dixon. Many early evangelists helped this church,
as well as J. H. Bicknell and C. B. Osgood of later days.

Just prior to 1913 B. H. Coonradt of Rochester traveled the
great distance to preach to this church once in two weeks. He
evidently did this in an effort to save the church, which
could no longer pay a pastor and, for a time, closed the Sunday
school. This condition was largely due to deaths and removals
of faithful members. The said record reads: "We have only
about twenty members, including children, only three adult
male members."

We remember, with Mrs. Bates, that Mr. and Mrs. Fred
Venables and their family and Mrs. Adele Finch were among
those who would not give up. There were others, we wish we
could think of them all. They met around the Lord's Table
regularly.

But a better day was to come. About two years later Burton
L. Hoffman was called as full-time minister. He took his bride
there during his ministry and they gave their usual good
service. Following them Rob Roy Hardin, afterward minister
at Lake Harriet, Minneapolis, spent the summer of 1917 as
minister.

About this time someone left money to the church, with
which the building was improved and the house next door to
it bought and remodeled as a parsonage. Mr. and Mrs. Harry
J. Hill were called in the fall of 1917 and they remained with
the church, giving fine leadership, for three years. It is interesting that Homer E. Hill, their son, now minister of the
Arlington Christian Church, Riverside, California, was born
in that parsonage and proudly exhibited it to us on our visit to
them.

PLAINVIEW

The present minister is a Minnesota man, Erwin Marshall, graduate of the Minnesota Bible College. Since the church no longer reports to the state office we have no recent report of membership. Mr. Marshall always gives good service.

One person never to be forgotten in this church is a woman who was blind for years. We knew her as Grandma McGilvary. She liked to have the ministers who came to her bedside kneel, while she placed her hands on their heads. Her prayers for God's blessing upon their labors have been a benediction to many ministers. She and her daughter, Sarah, out of small earnings, gave to their church and the work of missions in true pioneer fashion.

So the Plainview church has lived in the memory of many ministers and of the state servants. May it continue and prosper.

PLEASANT GROVE
(Olmsted County)

It has long been conceded that the Pleasant Grove church was the first church organized in Minnesota. It is situated about twelve miles from the great Mayo Center—Rochester. It is a fine farming community. The pioneers in this section were people of good education, coming from the sturdy, godly, American folk of eastern states.

Close to the church, in the open country, is the Marion church. These two were closely knit in the early days. An early historian, possibly Mrs. T. T. Van Dolah, writes of these churches: "Back beyond the days of Indian wars, beyond the Civil War period and into the territorial days lead these records."

It was in June, 1856, that F. W. Grant led in organizing the Pleasant Grove church, in the home of Peter Radabaugh. Charter members were Peter Radabaugh, Sr., Peter Radabaugh, Jr., John Radabaugh, Calinda Radabaugh, Elizabeth and Julia Radabaugh, Andrew Lighten, John Collins, Margaret Parks, Mr. and Mrs. Aughnbaugh, David Overend, Matthew Dougherty, Mrs. Calinda Radabaugh, Jane Bonham and Mr. and Mrs. Workman. Peter Radabaugh, Sr., was elected elder and John Collins, deacon. They were devoted leaders.

The first meeting place was a schoolhouse. The present brick structure was not erected until 1868. This was a good

Pleasant Grove

beginning. By the time your historian saw the building, about 1910, there had been added new classrooms, pews, heating plant, lighting plant, a bell and chimes. There was also a parsonage with about one acre of land.

Among workers of that day were Mr. and Mrs. F. W. Parkinson, Mrs. David (Mary) Overend, who appears among our pioneers, the families of Margaret Bentley, J. D. Parks, I. Tilton, J. M. Clark, Walter Welsh, A. D. Ehrhard, J. W. Kendell and C. H. Leach. The Sunday school superintendent was Leslie Page and the president of the Woman's Missionary Society was Mrs. G. Fordham. Mrs. F. W. Parkinson and her daughter, Mrs. Jennie Scott, were leaders in the missionary work. We remember that their missionary offerings for one year amounted to $506. At that time, too, their Sunday school numbered over 100. Many of the above mentioned people afterward moved to Rochester and united with the church there.

Both Marion and Pleasant Grove churches are off the railroad and have had the problem of other open country churches. Among early ministers were A. P. Frost, T. T. Van Dolah, R. W. Woodside and J. A. Grice.

A story that has been preserved through the years is that Elder E. T. Grant of Iowa was reported to have arrived at Brownsville, Houston County; that "the brethren" wanted him to hold a meeting for them and they delegated David Overend to secure his services. In order to do this Mr. Overend walked seventy-five miles, but the meeting was held. This event probably was before the organization of the church.

Richard Dobson, a minister from England, served this church about 1911-1913. His daughter, Mrs. Gertrude Sackett, also gave great service. Both Mr. Dobson and his wife have the little Pleasant Grove cemetery as their last resting place.

Of later years the church has been supplied mainly by students of the Minnesota Bible College or a nonresident minister. After a brilliant history of cooperation in all our missionary effort the church, in later years, became "independent." However, many factors account for the smaller work of the present day.

Whatever may happen in the future, Pleasant Grove church will ever reach far and wide in her influence. Older folk look back to their sojourn in its friendly portals with gratefulness. Many of its children serve well in other churches.

RONNEBY

(Benton County)

Just fifty-one years ago, July 22, 1900, the Ronneby Church was organized by Evangelist H. E. Rossel. There were twenty-three charter members. On September 28, 1901, the building was dedicated.

We find the names of several persons well known in the brotherhood who have at some time preached to this little church as minister or evangelist. Among them are J. R. Golden, A. J. Hollingsworth, J. H. Shellenberger, C. R. Neil, M. P. Hayden, J. H. Bicknell and C. B. Osgood.

There has been no great growth possible for this church. About 1907 they shared a ministry with Browerville, Sackville M. Smith preaching for the two churches. Students of the Minnesota Bible College had ministered to them during later years.

SHARON CHURCH

(Le Sueur County)

This church was organized in 1870, the result of the preaching of Elder J. A. LeVan. Thomas Randall, one of five brothers, became the minister.

We are unable to find the date in which this church ceased to be. However, since many members mentioned on its charter roll afterward served in other churches, we think that roll should have a place in this history. They are: Sidney Randall, Jannett Randall, Limpoon King, Mary King, Nelson Arbuckle, Ida Arbuckle, Mrs. Hester Ziebarth, Bessie Jones, Flora Lloyd, John Mattier, Elizabeth Mattier, James Mattier, Martha Mattier, Lyda Wickham, Mervin Drenning, children of Sidney Randall, Osa Randall, Effie May Ziebarth, Eldora Dantheus.

The church was located near Le Sueur. We read that the "State Meeting" was held there on two occasions.

SIMPSON

(Olmsted County)

Late in the 19th century the Simpson Church was organized. In days of less modern transportation, when winter travel was almost impossible, Mr. and Mrs. A. A. Levan, whose home was in this little village, led in organizing the church. Their three

SIMPSON

daughters were married and bringing up families. Grace
Levan Pearson and Robert, her husband, were ardent workers,
as were Ida Levan Wilson and Henry, her husband, as well
as Hettie Levan Johnson and her children. There were few
members at any time and resident ministry was never possible.
Usually this point was served by the Pleasant Grove minister.

Those who led the church were earnest folk. They believed
in the whole missionary program of the brotherhood. Neighbors met with them in their missionary society. We have
addressed large numbers of people in their home meetings.

After the death of Mr. and Mrs. Levan and the removal of
some others to Rochester, the trustees of the church requested
that their building be sold and the proceeds be given to the
State Society. C. E. Burgess, a director of the society, served
on its behalf.

Without exception, the members of this church went either
into the Rochester or Pleasant Grove fellowship. Montford
Pearson, grandson of Ambrose Levan, serves as an elder in
the Rochester church. His family and others could count their
many years of Christian service.

STAPLES

(Todd County)

About 1914-1915, when Arthur Long and Hugh Cooper were
holding evangelistic meetings for the Minnesota Christian Missionary Society, Mr. Cooper advised with the Board that Staples
might be a good town in which to open a church. He had found
members of the Christian church in that place. He remained
some time in the town, ascertained that a building could be
bought and the work started in its own home.

Staples is a railroad center of the Northern Pacific Railroad.
Mr. Cooper's idea was to make this town a sort of headquarters
for our Todd County churches. Charter members were Mrs.
Clemens, Mr. and Mrs. John Bryant, Mr. and Mrs. J. L. Kann,
Ben Boostrom, Daniel Sutton and Mrs. Lulu Stolhanske.

With the help of the Minnesota Christian Missionary Society,
Mr. and Mrs. W. J. Carry were called to be ministers. Mr.
Carry had been brought up in nearby Batavia county. They
were graduates of Cotner College.

STAPLES

Mr. John Bryant who died quite recently was a great leader in this church, which seemed to have a future in early days. However, many times there have not been funds to keep a full-time minister. Like other Todd County churches, it has largely divorced itself from the State Board.

A. J. Marshall gave ministerial help after the close of Mr. Carry's ministry. Among other ministers who served are Emil Gustafson, two whose surnames only we have, Mr. Hill and Mr. Waddell, A. E. Hoskins, a layman and former elder of Audubon Park Church, Minneapolis, Olin Atwood and Albert Shade. They may not be a full list.

Chester A. Balf, a minister, came from this church. His son Leo is also a minister and his daughter Adeline, a Christian education worker.

Besides the State Board's help, this church had support from the American Christian Missionary Society and the Christian Woman's Board of Missions in its early days.

TAMARACK

(Aitkin County)

In 1920 Dr. S. T. Willis, ministering to our church in Duluth, went to Tamarack. He and Mrs. Willis had become interested in some land but, as usual, his primary interest was people. There they met Mr. and Mrs. W. S. Mayhall and their daughters, Dr. J. P. Snader, Mrs. H. L. Newby and Mrs. W. N. Kelly. These persons became part of the charter membership of a church that Dr. Willis organized and ministered to from 1920 to 1922. All of them had been members of the Christian Church in Illinois. With those already named and J. P. Snader, two daughters of Mrs. Kelly, Mamie B. and Orvis Nelson, Mr. and Mrs. J. M. Mundon, Mrs. Florence Frasier and C. F. Pence the church was organized. They rented a store building in which they met for a long time. The first elders were W. S. Mayhall, J. M. Mundon and C. F. Pence.

We remember preaching to them on a winter Sunday evening. Even the dogs could not be left out in the cold. In this truly one-room building, with not even a porch and with benches having no back rests, the children must be still and

TAMARACK

dogs lie quietly during the worship. It was reverent worship and the little room was a temple, because of the spirit of the people.

Their building was started during the ministry of Ole Nielsen. Since they, themselves, must provide the material and build it, the progress was slow. Most of the material came from the H. L. Newby property and Mr. Nielsen was a good carpenter. It was finally finished in 1937 and dedicated on August 15 of that year.

The ministry of Ole Nielsen was the longest in the history of the church, 1928-1934. Many times there has been no minister, but always the church has maintained a Sunday school and met at the Lord's Table.

Like many small churches, Tamarack has trained and sent out those who have carried the Christian message to other places.

Among others who have served the church are G. H. Cachiaras, Don Lawrence, William Yarlett, Louise Negus and David Schafer. Glen Randall, a student, was minister in October, 1950.

TRUMAN

(Martin County)

In 1901 at the close of the International Convention, Leslie Wolfe, who was minister at Lewisville and Willow Creek, took an evangelist named Oliver to the home of Harry Fuller, suggesting the holding of a meeting, that a Church of Christ might be founded in Truman.

This meeting seems to have begun in the Baptist church, but the final part of it was held in a lodge hall. Another evangelist, J. O. Walton of Bloomington, Illinois, held a meeting later. The church was organized with the following charter members: Mr. and Mrs. H. A. Fuller, Mrs. J. Spencer, Mrs. Grace Fletcher, Mr. and Mrs. R. D. Parks, Mrs. N. D. True, Mrs. Gladys McLaughlin, Mr. and Mrs. Harry Winters, Clara Winters and Emma Winters.

The first minister was William Baier, who came from Winona and who also preached at Horicon. Evangelist C. Ray Murphy held a meeting which resulted in some additions. Bruce Black preached for a short time.

TRUMAN

The church held together for some time without a building, though a lot was bought. They met sometimes in a hall and for a time in the Methodist church, which was not having services. When there was no minister they kept up the Sunday school, the superintendent of which was H. A. Fuller.

Other ministers and evangelists, prior to the dedication of the church building, were J. P. Childs, Percy Atkinson and J. M. Dickson. The state evangelists, J. H. Bicknell and C. R. Neal, also gave guidance and held meetings.

The church, a pleasant and commodious building, was dedicated in the Fall of 1905. A former Baptist minister, F. E. Day, was the dedication preacher. He had taken membership with the church during a meeting held by J. H. Bicknell.

By this time the membership of the church has grown and there were many loyal workers: the Hiram and William Wallace families, the Arby Jones family and Mrs. Griggs, the capable organist, and mother of Earl N. Griggs, now minister of Central Christian Church in Pasadena. The I. J. Scribner family and others made the church a busy and hopeful place.

J. F. Ainsworth was minister in 1906 and he was followed by Alden Lee Hill, in 1907. Mr. Hill was minister two years and was followed by F. S. Halton. W. O. King gave some help to the church when he was minister of Horicon church, 1911-1918. Many unavailing attempts were made in early days to have the Baptist church and the Church of Christ come together.

In the early twenties, when Roland Wilder was minister, a beautiful parsonage was built on the lot beside the church, making a very complete setting for the comfort of the minister and the work of the church.

Students of the Minnesota Bible College have been among the ministers in later years. The present minister is Waldo E. Brown, who has preached for many years and whose recent pastorate is Worthington.

WHITE BEAR LAKE

(Ramsey County)

The First Church, St. Paul, and students of the Minnesota Bible College led toward the organization of a church in the town of White Bear Lake, which is situated on a lake of the

WHITE BEAR LAKE

same name. It is largely a summer resort town. An officer
and leader since the organization is L. E. Mills, formerly of
Garden City, Minnesota, and an ardent Christian layman. The
first section of the building was finished and services were held
November 14, 1943.

The church has not a large membership, but a good program
of work. At the present time Miss Pheraba Hoskins, graduate
and instructor of the Minnesota Bible College, is minister.
The Sunday school has an estimated membership of seventy-
five.

WILLOW CREEK)
(Blue Earth County)

The *Year Book* carries a line each year which speaks to us of
the loyalty of a group of missionary women. It is "Willow
Creek W.M.S." Then the annual *Year Book* lists their offerings.

On a beautiful spot, five miles from the town of Amboy, the
church was organized July 9, 1885, by Edwin Rogers of Mankato. An interesting sidelight on Mr. Rogers' career is told in
the church's history, as follows: "He was county superintendent
of schools and a preacher true to the Word." The organization took place in the Kinner schoolhouse.

Charter members were Mr. and Mrs. W. J. Chamberlain,
Mr. and Mrs. Ezra Cooper, Mrs. John Brown, Nellie Brown,
Edna Brown, Mrs. J. M. Stevens, Mrs. J. E. Salisbury, Julia
Wilder, Mrs. L. J. Wilder and E. P. Wilder.

For many years this church associated with Lewisville or
Garden City for ministry, usually having afternoon services.
When it seemed difficult, after much faithful planning, to give
the children of the families the sort of Sunday school they
should have, the members preferred to travel to near-by
churches. Most of the active ones chose Garden City.

Among the names of ministers we find that of Leslie Wolfe,
later missionary to the Philippines, who served for three years.
He served Lewisville as well.

One thinks of the Emmett Wilder and the H. O. Thompson
families as long-time leaders in this church. A son of the
Wilder family is Roland, minister at Madelia. From Mr.
Wilder we learn that the church once had 151 members.

WILLOW CREEK

At the time Mr. and Mrs. Lowell McPherson led this church in a meeting; about 1922, the missionary society had ceased to function.

Mr. McPherson reorganized it, the members being farm neighbors, many of whom were not members of the church. This society became a vital factor in neighborhood life. It decided to continue after the sale of the building. The meetings are still held once each month and the women always reach the aim set financially at the year's end.

CHURCHES OF A LATER DATE

Three churches, called "Church of Christ," were organized in recent years. We think the Southwest and Southeast Districts may have taken some responsibility and that the Minnesota Bible College helped in supplying their ministry. They are:

CANNON FALLS, GOODHUE COUNTY

This church was functioning before 1945, when your historian left Minnesota. We do not know whether it has a building, but there has been ministry. The State office has no reports, but the minister named in the *Year Book* is Wayne Armstrong, resident in Cannon Falls. This town is a busy, attractive place, not far from Red Wing.

PIPESTON, PIPESTONE COUNTY

We wish we could say more of this work. It is a good county seat town. It is probably of earlier date than Cannon Falls. Paul Millard when he was minister at Worthington took an interest in it. A resident minister's name is given as Walter A. Jones.

TRACY, LYON COUNTY

Many years ago we had on our "Scattered Disciples" list persons of Tracy and Marshall, the latter place being the county seat of Lyon County. We visited these people and we were not encouraged by them to attempt organization. The Southwest District led in organizing this church, we are told, about the same time as Pipestone. No reports are in the State Office. The *Year Book* names the minister as Homer Dobson.

EARLY DISCONTINUED CHURCHES

This history cannot be complete without remembering some of the places in which there were churches in past years, many of them having great influence in the State work. Some of these we have already recorded. Here are the others of which we know.

MORRISTOWN, Rice County, is mentioned as having been the place of the "State Meeting" in 1863. Mrs. T. T. Van Dolah mentions in her records of 1913 that this was a great convention, at which $624 was received in pledges to send T. T. Van Dolah and A. P. Frost out to evangelize. Although the State Society was not a corporation until 1877 the Morristown convention evidently adopted a constitution and by-laws, by which they established an orderly procedure for their work. We do not find a record of a building in Morristown.

BELLE PLAINE, Scott County. This church was never known as one of our people in the memory of your historian. However, some other communion offered to buy its building about 1942. They appealed to the State Board. As we remember, Forrest L. Richeson acted for the Board.

DASSEL, Meeker County and MONTROSE, Wright County, both had churches of fairly early organization. When only one family was left in the latter church they appealed to the State Society to take care of the building. J. R. Everett officiated for the Board. We know nothing of a Dassel building.

OLIVIA, county seat of Renville County, had an organization and a building prior to 1900. Their organization failed and their building was turned over to the State Society.

There are many other places, particularly in Southeast and Southwestern Minnesota where groups of Disciples met in early days. We think we have remembered all the places in which our people were organized as a church for any considerable period.

Wherever we have mentioned the sale of a building the reader will know that in all cases funds therefrom were put into the Permanent Fund of the State Society, and that to this day they remain there.

Later Discontinued Churches

INTERNATIONAL FALLS, County Seat of Koochiching County, was a place in which the State Board tried to establish work about 1912. They had a very small basement building. For ministry the church cooperated with Fort Francis, Ontario, Canada. Ross Musgrave was called as minister. He did a courageous work, against great odds. After about two years we were obliged to abandon this field.

JACKSON, Jackson County Seat, was organized by the Southwest District, but chiefly under the wing of the Worthington Church. There was a small building. Your historian once visited this church, which was quite small. The Worthington Church made an heroic attempt to see that there was ministry, but at length gave up the struggle.

WILLMAR, County Seat of Kandiyohi County, was the place of an attempted church about the early twenties. A tabernacle was built. As we remember, Litchfield, Redwood Falls and some other churches were interested. The State Board did not start this work, but tried to cooperate with it. Because of too great difficulties the work was abandoned after a short time.

Surely all these attempts must have their own fruitage, since earnest Christian preaching was heard.

And Finally

"We" and "Our" in the History of the Minnesota churches are not editorial terms; those words belong to all of us and to our common work of FAITH through the years.

To your historian the days of writing have been days of Christian fellowship. Many times friends have written: "How goes the book?" or "When will the history be ready?" They have assured me of their prayers; so have we worked together.

Faces and voices have come into this quiet room, far away from Minnesota. Great souls, living in this world and departed from it, have motivated the task of over a year. The "Crowd of Witnesses" (Goodspeed's translation) have given consolation, inspiration and faith day by day.

But there has been sorrow, too, for into the story has come the tragedy of division. The loving fellowship of many has been withdrawn from the common State task. My heart wants to cry out: "Do we always have to walk in two separate paths, we churches of the North Star State?"

The prayer, greater than all prayers, as this final word is said, is that Minnesota churches may find their way back to unity; that unity which began to be lost about 1920. The pioneers were people of strong opinions; they voiced these opinions freely but they believed in Jesus Christ and each other and stayed together.

Let us remember the old slogan: "In essentials unity, in nonessentials liberty, and in all things charity." The pioneers often said that; in fact, they taught it to me.

*"Now may the God of peace, that brought again from the dead our Lord Jesus, that great shepherd of the sheep, through the blood of the everlasting covenant, make you perfect in every good work to do His will, working in you that which is well-pleasing in his sight, through Jesus Christ; to whom be glory forever and ever. Amen."

*Hebrews 13:20, 21.

Acknowledgments

To the late Frank H. Mellen, of Minneapolis, we owe our deep gratitude. Mr. Mellen believed that a history of Minnesota churches ought to be written. We knew he was collecting material constantly. Between the years of 1923 and 1928 he urged your historian to start this work. There would have been no way of giving the leaders of the State Board through out the years had it not been for Mr. Mellen's records. Entries seem to have been made up to 1934.

Other records which had been included in Mr. Mellen's material were collected by Mrs. David Owen Thomas, C. B. Osgood and Miss Lida Beebe. These seem to have been prepared for an address given by Mrs. Thomas in 1913, in the State Convention at Antler's Park, Minnesota.

Photographs that are invaluable because of their inscriptions and dates also were collected by Mr. Mellen and Mr. Osgood. To J. R. Everett, layman, Minneapolis, and Vernon S. Stagner, State Executive Secretary, we express thanks for their careful preservation of Mr. Mellen's records. Also to Mr. Everett for his kindness in checking legal documents through the years, and to Mr. Stagner for his great help in getting records from local churches.

For booklets made available—St. Paul Church compiled by Mrs. J. S. Leavitt; Portland Avenue Church, Minneapolis, for the history written by the late Dr. David Owen Thomas; Garden City, by Edna M. Fellows, minister in 1933; also Audubon Park and Lake Harriet, from Mrs. Otto Johnson and J. R. Everett; Forest Lake, compiled by Don Lawrence, minister, and Redwood Falls from Mrs. George Huhnerkoch.

To Dr. Frank H. Marshall of Phillips University for making available his valuable records of the Minnesota Christian Education Association and Northwestern Christian College. Also to Carroll H. Lemon, minister of Lincoln, Nebraska, for material preserved by his mother, Mary Clipfell Lemon of the same college. To G. H. Cachiaras for his great help in providing catalogues and other material of the Minnesota Bible College.

To more church folk than it is possible to mention for prompt answers to letters sent to them by the State office and the historian.

ADA L. FORSTER
Oakland, California

135

Index